Cambridge Elements

Elements in Global Urban History
edited by
Michael Goebel
Graduate Institute Geneva
Tracy Neumann
Wayne State University
Joseph Ben Prestel
Freie Universität Berlin

EPIDEMIC CITIES

Antonio Carbone
German Historical Institute in Rome

CAMBRIDGE
UNIVERSITY PRESS

Shaftesbury Road, Cambridge CB2 8EA, United Kingdom

One Liberty Plaza, 20th Floor, New York, NY 10006, USA

477 Williamstown Road, Port Melbourne, VIC 3207, Australia

314–321, 3rd Floor, Plot 3, Splendor Forum, Jasola District Centre,
New Delhi – 110025, India

103 Penang Road, #05–06/07, Visioncrest Commercial, Singapore 238467

Cambridge University Press is part of Cambridge University Press & Assessment,
a department of the University of Cambridge.

We share the University's mission to contribute to society through the pursuit of
education, learning and research at the highest international levels of excellence.

www.cambridge.org
Information on this title: www.cambridge.org/9781108930895

DOI: 10.1017/9781108946292

First published 2022

A catalogue record for this publication is available from the British Library.

ISBN 978-1-108-93089-5 Paperback
ISSN 2632-3206 (online)
ISSN 2632-3192 (print)

Cambridge University Press & Assessment has no responsibility for the persistence
or accuracy of URLs for external or third-party internet websites referred to in this
publication and does not guarantee that any content on such websites is, or will
remain, accurate or appropriate.

Epidemic Cities

Elements in Global Urban History

DOI: 10.1017/9781108946292
First published online: September 2022

Antonio Carbone
German Historical Institute in Rome

Author for correspondence: Antonio Carbone, antonio.carbone@posteo.de

Abstract: *Epidemic Cities* provides an overview of the history of epidemics through a particular focus on a range of cities in different regions of the world. The dual focus on both epidemics and specific cities provides an unusual perspective on global history: the analysis of globally circulating epidemics enables reconstructing a variety of wide-reaching entanglements, on the one hand. On the other hand, the concentration with specific urban settings highlights differences and the unevenness engendered by global entanglements. After an introduction concerning the history of the relationship between medicine, epidemics, and cities, the book focuses on the history of three epidemic diseases and how they affected Paris, Buenos Aires, Hong Kong, Bombay, and Baltimore. The timings of major pandemics punctuate the structure of the book: cholera pandemics from the 1830s to the late nineteenth century, bubonic plague at the turn of the twentieth century, and finally tuberculosis until the mid-twentieth century.

Keywords: urban history, global history, history of medicine, epidemics, modern history

ISBNs: 9781108930895 (PB), 9781108946292 (OC)
ISSNs: 2632-3206 (online), 2632-3192 (print)

Contents

Introduction

In the wake of the COVID-19 pandemic, medical experts, especially in disciplines such as epidemiology and virology, have suddenly become protagonists on the mainstream media scene. Their contributions in newspapers and appearances on television, on radio, and at official press conferences have reached a status of ubiquity. Unexpectedly, technical concepts such as 'basis reproduction number' along with a wealth of graphs showing present and predicted developments of the pandemic have left their traditionally small scholarly audience to transform into issues widely discussed by the general public. Apart from medical experts, columnists and social scientists have also engaged in constructing countless scenarios that attempt to gauge the possible outcomes of COVID-19 on societies, connecting the effort to understand the present with the will to predict the future.

This Element has been written in the context of this essential need to grasp the current issues of COVID-19 while forecasting outcomes; the question concerning the specific contribution of history and especially the history of epidemics can legitimately be raised at this juncture. How can historians of epidemics contribute to discussions of present and perhaps future epidemics by looking at the past? Historians are indeed united by their interest in the past, a feature that may well render them suspiciously dubious forecasters. As a result, their scientific contributions can address neither the present nor the future but can be of relevance nonetheless. Historians cannot take part in current debates by providing answers, but they can certainly pose important and stimulating questions that can change the perspective on current events. As the historian Achim Landwehr argues in an essay on the critical impact of history, it is the distance between past and present that enables historians to shed light on central issues and thus question what exists (Landwehr 2012). By showing the varied impact of past epidemics on demographics, the environment, and urban space, for instance, historians can inspire questions that illuminate underexposed aspects of the present. Indeed, history provides an informed basis from which to interrogate the present, thereby influencing the future (Birn 2020; Green 2020a).

The historian of epidemics Jo Hays remarked that, despite the perceived simplicity of the questions historians ask when analysing past epidemics, the answers that follow are invariably complex and may even appear hesitant (Hays 2007). In fact, the kind of influence epidemics have had on past societies has been almost as varied as the number of the single epidemics and of contexts in which they broke out. To provide an example, answers to a classic question concerning the way in which epidemics have affected public authorities might sound rather indecisive. As Jo Hays convincingly reports, major epidemics have nearly always had an impact on public authorities, but the quality of this impact has greatly depended on a number of variables that are extremely challenging to account for. At times, epidemics reinforced the power of public authorities, such as instances in which they assumed extra powers to carry out more invasive forms of social control. On the other hand, epidemics have also destabilised public authorities, whose actions inspired fierce popular resistance after they enforced strict containment measures. In other settings, epidemics have given rise to power struggles between different authorities, such as disputes between local and national as well as religious and political authorities. What is more, these three possible outcomes on public authorities are not mutually exclusive and can occur in the same place at the same time. As with the example concerning the impact of epidemics on public authorities, many other issues in the history of epidemics cannot be tackled with straightforward answers.

However, historians can point to issues that have been relevant in past epidemics that could be overlooked in the present. For instance, again concerning the example of the influence of epidemic crises on public authorities, historians can highlight the fact that nearly all of the major epidemics in history have had a decisive impact on the development of public authorities. A similar argument can be made to gauge the influence of epidemics on cities. Their influence on densely inhabited human settlements is varied and depends on innumerable variables; nevertheless, it is possible to affirm that epidemics have had an almost invariably significant impact on urban centres. This may not allow for any noteworthy future predictions, but it does enable the formation of more informed questions. Against this backdrop, this Element aims to provide readers with a brief guide that serves as a starting point to explore the rich literature on the history of epidemics in cities and, albeit indirectly, to engage in a critical questioning of the present from this vantage point.

The overview provided in this Element is intended to highlight certain salient trends of the impact of single epidemics on a wide range of cities in the past two centuries. In some cases, an analysis of a single epidemic therefore focuses on a short time frame and on the reconstruction of the events and certain changes those events inspired. The idea behind this way of regarding epidemics is essentially their framing as moments that trigger exceptional, decisive, and long-lasting changes in societies. However, epidemics are not only catastrophes that can spur sudden and surprising reactions. They are also, as several social historians have noted (Briggs 1961; Evans 1988; McGrew 1965), crises that '[unsettle] the normal functioning of society and [bring] to the surface latent social antagonisms' (Durey 1979, 1). Analysing epidemics from this perspective, conceiving them as moments that have exacerbated already existing conflicts, also facilitates the identification of central structural traits of societies which are otherwise rendered almost invisible in their normal functioning. In other words, as Charles Rosenberg puts it, epidemics constitute for the social scientist 'an extraordinarily useful sampling device' (Rosenberg 1989, 2). If some of the cases presented in this Element rely mostly on the first idea, of epidemics as decisive events, others prefer to use the approach of framing epidemics as revealing moments that enable historians to focus on conflicts concerning long-lasting processes. Though they may appear to varying extents in the cities examined here, these two ways of framing epidemics are present in every case analysis in this Element as it attempts to bring together these non-contradictory forms of conceiving epidemics.

Cities – the other big focus of this Element – as much as epidemics provide an especially fruitful vantage point to look at questions concerning global history. If epidemics can be conceived of as a temporal 'sampling device' that enables identifying in a compressed time frame some central tenets of societies as well as moments of decisive change, I regard cities as spaces where various central discussions and conflicts played out. Cities were not only often the gateway from which epidemic diseases entered larger territorial units or not. They were also 'critical junctures of globalization' where processes happening at different scales – for instance, on the global, regional, national, and local levels – intertwined and clashed (Middell and Naumann 2010, 6). This is not meant to deny rural spaces – as opposed to urban ones – their role as places of (dis) entanglement. However, cities played in many cases a specific role in the history of globalisation. As Frederick Cooper argues, 'the world has long been – and still is – a space where economic and political relations are very uneven; it is filled with lumps, places where power coalesces surrounded by those where it does not' (Cooper 2001, 190). Cities functioned often as these very spatial 'lumps' (Goebel 2018) where power concentrated, making them a spatial 'sampling device'. This allows looking not only at the processes of connection and entanglement, which global historians have often highlighted in past decades, but also at the frictions and sometimes the processes of disentanglement that arise from the uneven and conflictual nature of globalisation and crystallise at the 'small' urban scale.

The specific impact epidemic crises have had on cities is mainly filtered through the way in which they were interpreted by those who experienced them. The first section of this Element therefore deals with the ever-changing array of viewpoints from which epidemic diseases have been conceived and with the ways in which these conceptions acted on the responses of cities, their authorities, and inhabitants to epidemic outbreaks. Medicine has played a central role in defining the evolution of conceptions of epidemic diseases, and the first section reconstructs certain key turning points in the history of the relationship between medicine, epidemics, and cities. It opens with the theories of Hippocrates, which substantially influenced the understanding of disease well into the nineteenth century, and ends with the rise of the germ theory of disease in the late nineteenth century.

The following three sections focus on cholera, the plague, and tuberculosis, three major epidemic diseases at the root of a series of pandemics that affected several cities across the globe during the nineteenth and twentieth centuries. Emerging for the first time at the beginning of the nineteenth century, cholera was the first epidemic disease to be clearly viewed by contemporaries as being of a global magnitude. The second section of this Element begins with a general introduction on cholera, the salient traits of its history, and certain essential features of the disease's historiography. Following this introduction, the section focuses on the cholera outbreaks in Paris and Buenos Aires. The core of the analysis of the Parisian epidemic revolves around the riots that took place during Paris' first cholera outbreak in 1832. In its conclusion, the analysis of the Parisian case suggests that these riots represented a novelty with an outcome that was relevant for the approach to the reform of the French capital in the following decades. The case of the cholera epidemics in Buenos Aires during the late 1860s shows how the disease triggered a far-reaching debate on the presence of meat factories in the city, on the future of the city itself, and on its position in the Atlantic world. Facts aside, a range of fantasies concerning the strategies adopted by Western European cities such as Paris and London to tackle cholera were among the elements at the root of this debate. The Parisian experience in tackling cholera influenced the elites of Buenos Aires, but only after extensive filtering and mediation through the constellation of local values and interests. The central tenet connecting the two examples revolves around an analysis of the influence, in a rather unexpected fashion, of the first case, Paris, on the more recent one, Buenos Aires.

The third section, on the plague, resembles the preceding section on cholera in terms of structure. The section begins with a general introduction to some key themes discussed in the huge corpus of historiography on the plague, which focuses, however, mainly on the Black Death in the fourteenth century and plague epidemics in early modern Europe. The section then presents further plague epidemics at the turn of the twentieth century in Hong Kong and Bombay, both under British colonial rule at the time. The sections on these two cities highlight similarities and contrasts between both cases. The symbolic investment in Hong Kong and Bombay by the British empire differed some-what; whereas Hong Kong was establishing itself as a commercial hub, Bombay was portrayed as a showcase of modernity in British India. A disease considered a shameful relic of the past, the plague was blamed squarely on the local populations in both cases, among which most of those who perished were to be found. In both cases, the local populations reacted to the measures ordered by the colonial authorities with protests. Forced to confront such opposition in Hong Kong and Bombay alike, the British authorities backed down and acknowledged the demands of the local population. When the height of the crisis had passed, however, they proceeded to carry out violent slum clearings, which mainly targeted the poor among the urban population.

While the previous sections focus on diseases that were characterised by both an immense emotional impact and comparatively short temporalities that ranged between a few months and a few decades, the fourth section, on tuberculosis, presents a disease that had been virtually continuously present for thousands of years and inspired varying reactions in a range of societies. Throughout most of the nineteenth century, tuberculosis was widely perceived as an individual non-contagious condition and therefore failed to inspire far-reaching emotional and political reactions. As new theories concerning the contagious nature of the disease rose in the 1880s, tuberculosis gradually transformed into an epidemic that was viewed with great concern at the beginning of the twentieth century. After the general introduction, the section highlights the cases of Baltimore and Buenos Aires, assessing the ways in which the fight against tuberculosis intersected with traditions and tendencies towards urban racial and ethnic segregation. In the case of Baltimore, the racial segregation of African Americans intensified the outbreak of tuberculosis, while being simultaneously used to further underpin the existence of racial boundaries. In the case of Buenos Aires, a city that was not segregated along similar ethnic and racial lines at the outset of the emergence of tuberculosis, the disease did not have a great influence on the distribution patterns of the population.

The dual focus of this Element on global epidemics and specific cities facilitates greater insight into transnational processes such as pandemics and their localisation in a variety of contrasting settings. This study creates possibilities for comparative analyses between different cities, such as the cases of Hong Kong and Bombay, and Baltimore and Buenos Aires. Furthermore, it shows how cities could influence each other; in the case of Paris and Buenos Aires, the former mostly influenced the latter, though in a somewhat unexpected and indirect fashion. In the context of phenomena such as pandemics, a focus on cities can give rise to a gauging of the uneven impact of global processes in different local contexts. By simultaneously concentrating on global phenomena and globally connected cities, this Element highlights similarities and differences in global connections while also underlining their non-linear and asymmetrical character, deliberately muddying the waters of what can at times be an oversimplified narrative of global history. In fact, if the success of global history has spurred historians into looking beyond the framework of the nation, the enthusiasm for the global has occasionally developed into a scholarly mannerism that is often satisfied with the detection of ubiquitous entanglements, often underplaying both the absence of connections and their rather conflicting nature (Goebel 2016).

1 Epidemics, Medicine, and Cities

Before the emergence of the social sciences between the end of the nineteenth century and the beginning of the twentieth, a development which gave rise to specific urban disciplines such as urban sociology and planning, medical doctors and hygienists were the central experts in the field of the urban. Medicine had become the pivotal knowledge system that people relied upon both to make sense of disease and to envision anti-epidemic reforms, especially concerning epidemic outbreaks in cities, a circumstance that was certainly not uncommon. Even after the rise of specific urban disciplines, medicine has been a central scientific arena in which not only disease and its causes were discussed; regulations were also drafted regarding the way people should live and construct their environment in order to prevent disease. This section focuses on how different medical traditions and schools, which are typically identified as the Western predecessors of today's hegemonic biomedicine, viewed the epidemics and the relationship between disease and the ways in which human beings lived in cities. The Element focuses on a specific genealogy of modern biomedical thought that gravitates towards the Western history of thought and starts its narration with the humoral medicine of the ancient physicians Hippocrates and Galen, which served as the dominant medical thought in Europe until the nineteenth century.

Prior to analysing the history of these medical schools and conceptions, important clarifications must be made concerning the concept of modern biomedicine and especially its relationship with the Western medical tradition. Providing a clear definition of modern biomedicine is a daunting task because biomedicine does not exist as a coherent and homogenous body of knowledge. In fact, numerous medical traditions from different world regions have conflicted, juxtaposed, cooperated, and intermingled in creating today's hegemonic, even though highly disputed, biomedical understanding (Cook 2018; Jackson 2018). For instance, looking at Europe in the early Middle Ages, it is impossible to distinguish 'Western' medicine from an alleged 'Islamic' counterpart: Islamic physicians studied and translated the work of ancient Greek physicians and also drew from a number of other traditions, eventually spreading this knowledge throughout the Mediterranean region and well beyond (Ebrahimnejad 2018). More recently, 'Western' and 'Chinese' medicine have constructed a deep relationship of exchange; modern Chinese medicine results from a conflation of Chinese and Western practices and knowledge. Conversely, in numerous regions across the world, traditional East Asian practices such as acupuncture are widely accepted and applied (Lo and Stanley-Baker 2018). Not only are regional boundaries between medical traditions often rather artificial, but medical epistemologies can also vary consistently. For instance, what we might understand as Western medicine has also been contested from within the controversial boundaries of the Western tradition: homeopathy, for instance, a medical school established in Germany in the eighteenth century, has opposed scientific Western medicine and managed to survive and thrive to this day (Volf and Aulas 2019). Therefore, as these examples show, modern biomedicine is the result of long-lasting processes of entanglement and exchange between different medical traditions at different levels. When using the terms 'medicine' or 'Western medicine' in this Element, I tend to endow them with more consistency and coherence than they have ever really possessed. The reader should bear in mind that I use these terms as a type of shortcut to illustrate an otherwise rather chaotic set of ideas.

As a result of these clarifications, the reader might question why I include a section on the history of Western medicine and its interpretations of the relationship between epidemic disease and the urban environment. The answer lies in the specific time frame and range of cities considered in this Element. Even though medicine developed through 'trials, encounters, and appropriations overseas' and has always been a field of hybridisation and contestation (Arnold 1996, 11), in the cases analysed in this Element, Western medicine represented the common language of the ruling elites and functioned as a contested but nonetheless hegemonic language. In fact, notwithstanding the constant contaminations between different medical traditions, the language of Western medicine has progressively risen to occupy a position of dominance among other systems of medical knowledge. A central reason for this path certainly lies in the history of colonialism: as the European empires came to dominate vast swathes of the globe, they developed knowledge systems, medicine among them, that played a fundamental role in colonial rule. The specific focus of this study lies on cities that largely maintained a direct connection with colonialism and imperialism. For instance, Paris as a metropolitan capital, Bombay as a colonial centre, and Buenos Aires as the capital of a postcolonial nation, Argentina, all formed part of an entangled colonial world, albeit with evidently contrasting roles, in which the language and practices of Western medicine served as tools of colonial knowledge and power.

This does not mean that medicine was a mere imposition from the centres to the imperial peripheries; it was in fact a hybrid construction. However, it is also important not to overlook that the processes of mutual appropriation and contamination took place in the context of asymmetrical power relations in which imperial agents often occupied positions of power. Leaving aside the ambition of writing an '*histoire totale*' of medical knowledge, epidemics, and cities, in the following sections I explicitly deal with a Western genealogy of medical knowledge and nevertheless highlight, starting from this vantage point, the constitutive character of colonial encounters for the formation of medical thought and practices.

1.1 Humoral Medicine and Miasma

An analysis of the history of medicine, its conceptions of disease, and their relationship with cities begins here with humoral medicine. This is not the case because all conventional histories of Western thought commence in ancient Greece, but rather because this form of medicine was the main reference point for physicians in Europe, South Asia, and the Mediterranean region for thousands of years and played a central role as the basis for explanations of epidemic disease that did not revolve around the idea of contagion. Humoral medicine dominated the scene for an impressively long period from the fifth century BCE well into the nineteenth century CE, despite being the object of a great number of differing and contrasting interpretations such as that of Galen, who became its main interpreter during late antiquity. Its origin goes back to the sixty treaties written by the Greek physician Hippocrates and his followers. The corpus of Hippocratic texts is organised around a central principle, namely that disease is an event of nature that can be explained and treated through natural means. Hippocratic physicians did not resort to supranatural and divine powers to explain the body, its health, and its afflictions. Following the view of the natural origin of the human body, Hippocratic medical philosophy conceived a system of analogies and correspondences between what was then understood as the macrocosms of the universe and the microcosm of the human body.

According to Hippocrates, universe and body were made of the same elements and governed by the same natural laws. The Hippocratic conception of elements of nature was directly borrowed from the teachings of the ancient Greek philosopher Aristotle. They regarded the body as being governed by four fluids – the 'humours' – which corresponded to the four 'terrestrial' elements theorised by Aristotle. The black bile matched earth, the phlegm corresponded to water, the blood denoted air, and the yellow bile represented fire. In accordance with this doctrine, health was viewed as a balance of the fluids in the body. Disequilibrium or corruption of these bodily components resulted in disease. In keeping with such ideas, discrete diseases such as tuberculosis or influenza did not exist. On the contrary, each different manifestation of the body was a symptom of the essential condition of imbalance in the ratio of bodily humours (Nutton 2013).

The conception of illness as an imbalance of the single body lay at the root of the idea that disease was a non-transmittable condition of the individual, which in turn required an ad hoc therapy. Hippocratic medicine therefore did not regard epidemics as the result of a disease spreading through contact between individuals and instead provided other explanations for such events. In Hippocratic medicine, a defined set of causes had been established that could result in an imbalance of the humours and therefore disease. Certain causes only concerned individuals and their regimen: the intake of food and drink, the passions of the soul, and the quality of sleep and physical exercise. However, when an entire population became ill simultaneously, individual regimens could hardly be responsible and humoral physicians saw environmental factors as the primary causes. The environmental or external influences were mainly identified through the weather and air quality. In fact, air could become corrupted and poisonous according to the – using a modern term – 'humoralists', a so-called miasma. These miasmas, which could descend or rise in an entire city, caused the outbreak of epidemics. The source of the poisoning of the air had to be found in 'unpleasant smells descending from the stars, rising odours (from the earth or marshes), or fumes coming from decomposing cadavers' (Jouanna 2012, 125).

The fact that epidemic disease was intimately tied to certain locations in which these poisoning fumes descended, rose, and concentrated had important consequences for cities. Throughout the long period in which humoral medicine played a pivotal role in explaining disease, the conception that epidemics were elicited by a locally concentrated poisoning of the air meant that, as soon as an epidemic broke out, people were required to leave the contaminated area immediately. This also applied to cities, and Hippocratic physicians recommended that their patients leave the city and find a place with uncontaminated air. Sanctioned by humoral physicians, fleeing cities was a common reaction when major epidemics broke out, as in the so-called Plague of Athens in the fifth century BCE and, a thousand years later, in the Plague of Justinian (Little 2007). After antiquity, similar phenomena also occurred, such as in many cities during the fourteenth century CE, when bubonic plague swept across Eurasia, earning in Europe the name Black Death.

1.2 Contagion and Quarantine

The humoral idea of poisoned air as the source of disease was, however, not the only assertion in circulation. For instance, during classical antiquity, the tradition of magic-religious medicine viewed epidemic disease as the result of contact with contaminated people and objects, in partial opposition to Hippocratic medicine. Both regarded miasma as the origin of epidemic disease but perceived it in contrasting fashion. In religious tradition, miasma was not poisoned air but a 'stain', a fault of the individual or the community. This kind of miasma was highly contagious and, for instance, even the ritual instruments used for the purification of the sick were believed to carry the miasma and needed to be taken as far away from the community as possible (Jouanna 2012). Furthermore, the strict isolation reserved for lepers as described in the Bible, for instance, points to a notion of epidemic disease as the result of contact between human beings. Despite their opposing positions on the subject, the humoral-miasmatic and religious-contagious conceptions of epidemic disease nonetheless had similar effects on cities. For humoral physicians, epidemics were tied to given places and fleeing from cities was therefore a sensible solution; likewise, for religious medicine that viewed cities as possible breeding grounds of contagious people and objects, leaving was a viable way for the individual to avoid infection. A relevant difference was notable, however; following the religious 'contagionist' notion, miasma could be erased through acts of purification and, more importantly, both humans and objects carrying the 'stain' could be isolated or kept outside the community, a procedure that became essential during the late Middle Ages, when bubonic plague hit Eurasia.

The simultaneous existence of different theories on the causation and spread of epidemic disease, as in the case of humoral-miasmatic and religious-contagious ideas, withstood the end of antiquity and became a constant of European medicine until the end of the nineteenth century. Even before the idea of contagion was scientifically revived in the sixteenth century by the physician Girolamo Fracastoro, cities on the European continent, which were regularly affected by bubonic plague from the fourteenth to the late eighteenth century during the so-called second plague pandemic, devised a system of preventive measures based on a mix of 'contagionist' and 'miasmatic' viewpoints (Harrison 2012). One of the key ideas lay in the consideration of disease as an external invasion, and anti-plague measures were primarily designed to prevent the penetration of disease into ports or cities. This conception was also intimately connected to the scale and structure of the commercial and port cities of the Italian peninsula, which were the hardest hit by the plague and therefore at the forefront of the establishment of anti-plague measures. The institutions of maritime quarantine, lazarettos, and sanitary cordons – words and concepts still widely in use today – represented the backbone of anti-plague systems. In what became an influential model, the city authorities in Venice ordered the construction of two institutions (Lazzaretto Nuovo and Vecchio) during the fifteenth century on islands in the Venetian lagoon. Ships arriving from ports in which plague had been reported were not allowed to enter the city and had to dock in one of the lazaretto islands. As contagious human beings and possible miasmas had to be dissipated, crews, passengers, and merchandise were required to remain isolated from the city for forty days (the word *quarantine* has its roots in the Italian word for forty, *quaranta*) (Crawshaw 2012).

Moving away from its original maritime and city-state context, the practice of quarantine and the general idea of isolation migrated during the early modern period to other institutions, such as states and empires. In these cases, the principle of keeping disease beyond city walls or outside ports was adapted to the scale of large overland geographical and population units. A system functioning under the name of sanitary cordon consisted of military enforcement of regional borders, a whole state, or an empire to keep out supposedly diseased foreigners. The most striking example of this strategy was probably the eastern border of the Habsburg empire, which was in constant operation from the early eighteenth to the late nineteenth century. The so-called Military Border functioned through a complex system of peasant conscription from different ethnic groups who carried out policing tasks in the border regions. From the Adriatic to today's Romania, the Military Border was dotted with forts and quarantine stations and connected to an intelligence network that sent information on epidemic outbreaks in the eastern Mediterranean to Vienna, the capital of the empire (Ágoston 1998).

Sanitary cordons could have important consequences for cities. In fact, unlike city states, an overland state could decide to confine cities within cordons and prevent inhabitants from leaving. Equally, within the city, people identified as diseased or as possible sources of disease could be forced to remain locked in their homes or forced into enclosed public institutions. Returning to the case of Venice, lazarettos also played a central role in this context. Those suspected of having been infected with the plague or deemed non-compliant with anti-plague regulations were brought to one of the lazaretto islands. Since no effective cure for the plague existed, entering a lazaretto was often viewed as a death sentence and injunctions to be transferred into one were often met with fierce resistance.

The prompt recovery and disposal of corpses was another key task typically carried out by city authorities during epidemics. If the idea of quarantine was mostly based on a contagious conception of disease, the disposal of corpses rested on a miasmatic notion of disease. Decomposing corpses were, in fact, regarded as one of the primary sources of the miasmas that poisoned the air and caused the disease to proliferate (Carmichael 1986). These were only some of the measures facing people living in plague-stricken cities. Individual cities opted to enforce their own regulations, such as the killing and disposal of all animals, or the prohibition to tan or generally practise activities suspected of creating miasmas. Epidemics also proved to be typical moments in which religious or ethnic minorities, especially the Jewish population in Europe, became the victims of sweeping and violent persecution and were accused of being responsible for the epidemics and expelled from the city, discriminated against, or killed. Against this backdrop, it is easy to understand why the mere rumour of pestilence could cause massive waves of people fleeing from cities and why, once sick, people often tended to conceal their illness to avoid being separated from their loved ones or, worse, declared guilty of aiding the spread of the disease.

1.3 The Hospital and Diseases As Discrete Entities

As an urban institution, the hospital was intimately connected with the conception of lazarettos as places where the sick were rounded up and isolated. This played an especially central role in the emergence of new conceptions of disease between the end of the eighteenth century and the beginning of the nineteenth. Whereas humoral medicine imagined the disequilibrium of the humours as the only disease at the root of all possible illnesses, the new theories, which had their main centre of propagation in Paris, instead regarded the existence of multiple diseases as specific discrete entities. This new assertion of disease was the outcome of almost three centuries of gradual estrangement from humoral theories and the epistemology on which these rested (Hannaway and La Berg 1998; Warner 2003). This progressive shift was rooted in both new scientific practices and approaches and the trailblazing novelties inspired by the experiences and contacts engendered by the European conquests on the American continent.

Concerning the new scientific practices, human dissection, for instance, which in Europe had only been practised clandestinely for centuries, gradually became in early modern Europe one of the elementary practices of the medical profession. In the sixteenth century, anatomists such as Andreas Vesalius and Gabriele Falloppio initiated new ways of understanding and representing the human body through drawings based on dissections (Carlino 1999). In physiology, new paradigms emerged; for instance, in the seventeenth century, the physician William Harvey developed a theory on the functioning of the circulatory system and demonstrated that the heart served as its pumping centre (Fuchs 2001). Moreover, a new understanding of nature questioned the foundations of Aristotelian natural science and with it the fundamental tenets of humoral medicine. For instance, the chemistry propagated by Antoine Lavoisier disproved Aristotle's theory of the four elements. New instruments such as thermometers and microscopes also changed both the epistemology and diagnostic options of medicine (Daston and Galison 2007). These shifting scientific paradigms were deeply connected with the overall sense of the coming of a new era prompted by colonialism and the deepening of contacts between the European, American, and African continents. For medicine, the contact with African and American populations meant a notable expansion of knowledge and the availability of new medical practices and ingredients (Hernández Sáenz 1997). Furthermore, the devastating epidemics caused by the arrival of Africans, Asians, and Europeans on the American continent brought the assumptions of the millennial tradition of humoral medicine under great scrutiny (Alchon 2003).

Each of these elements greatly contributed to a profound questioning of medical knowledge and the creation of new paradigms. Nonetheless, it may well have been the hospital and the great number of sick human bodies that Paris was able to provide that triggered a major shift in medical epistemology at the turn of the nineteenth century. Whereas Hippocratic medicine had always practised medicine by interpreting the disease of each patient in singular ways, the hospital changed the way physicians interacted with their patients. Situated in Paris, a city with a growing population and in an almost permanent state of war from the beginning of the French Revolution in 1789 until the end of the Napoleonic Wars in 1815, the larger state-controlled hospitals received huge numbers of patients. One of the great novelties of the Parisian system was a centralised spatial dislocation of the sick in different wards of the hospital, where patients were grouped according to the pattern of their symptoms. This initially rather bureaucratic principle of organising patients was one of the main elements that eventually gave rise to the assertion that diseases were distinct entities with distinguishable characteristics and courses (Weisz 2001). For example, the idea of phthisis (tuberculosis) and typhoid fever as discrete entities was partly the outcome of this system. Physicians from the Paris school were primarily preoccupied with describing and cataloguing diseases. For instance, they auscultated the lungs through their newly introduced stethoscopes and classified different pathologic respiratory sounds as wheezing, stridor, or crackling. If the practice of the Parisian physicians largely consisted of classifying rather than understanding the causes of disease, their contribution nonetheless played a key role in influencing the discussion on the causation of disease. Indeed, if diseases were different entities, each discrete disease could correspond to a specific set of causes.

The relationship between medicine and cities was also consistently transformed by the new medical theories inaugurated by the Paris School of Medicine at the turn of the nineteenth century. Firstly, the city delivered a high number of patients that enabled medical professionals to observe and describe diseases and their individual characteristics. If the Parisian main hospital, the Hôtel-Dieu, had not been in the very centre of a rapidly growing city, the implementation of this new system of classifying patients and diseases would have probably been impossible. Secondly, the new system of medical knowledge was not based on the observation of a single patient but rather on the observation of large numbers of patients, which shifted the attention of physicians onto questions of numerical correlation and prompted the advent of medical statistics. Analysing disease through statistics induced a change in the conception of hygiene and consequently in the way medicine envisioned its intervention in cities. Connected to the individualist tradition of humoral medicine, hygiene had essentially developed as a doctrine of diet and regimen. Regarding questions on large numbers of patients and their correlation with each other, the Paris School delivered the tools that facilitated the development of hygiene as a means of social intervention in the following years. If the physicians of the Paris School were not directly interested in questions on urban hygiene, they nevertheless introduced a statistical mode of medical knowledge that paved the way for a new understanding of hygiene as a social science, which in turn viewed the city as one of its main fields of application (Park 2018; Sarasin 2001).

1.4 The Sanitary Movement

The conception of the existence of singular diseases, the emergence of medical statistics, and the development of urban hygiene led to the observation in Europe that disease was connected to patients' social backgrounds and to the places in which they lived. Furthermore, the emergence of new diseases such as cholera, which began a dramatic expansion across the globe from the 1820s onwards, pushed physicians out of the hospital ward and into public streets and private residences. Searching for the causes of disease, medical doctors and newly created hygienists, who, as in the case of Edwin Chadwick, were not necessarily physicians, began to explore their cities and especially the neighbourhoods with the highest mortality rates. What they encountered was usually poverty, high-density working-class housing, 'filth', and the ubiquity of foul odours (Chevalier 1973; Corbin 1986). The foul stench provoked by waste, excrement, the decomposition of organic matter, and overcrowding appeared to these men – looking at the problem through the lenses of both the humoral tradition and the religious beliefs connecting miasma with sin and contagion – as the chief causes of epidemic diseases (Barnes 2006; Halliday 2001).

The therapy for the 'cleansing' of cities prescribed by leading figures of the 'sanitary movement' such as Louis-René Villermé, Thomas Southwood Smith, and Erwin Chadwick by the mid-nineteenth century consisted of a wide array of measures that can be summarised in two main points. Firstly, 'sanitarians' tried to tackle the problem of poverty, which they considered one of the main causes of 'filth' and therefore of disease. Representatives of the sanitary movement advocated for radical changes in the living conditions of urban workers and their families and for a substantial 'clean-up' of working-class neighbourhoods. Some among them, such as Chadwick, saw the origin of the material and hygienic misery of the urban working classes in their alleged immorality and laziness. Moreover, in the sanitarians' opinion, the miasmas the poor caused through their 'filthiness', which allegedly arose as a result of their moral intemperance, put the lives of the whole community, including respectable citizens, in danger (Hamlin 1998). These sanitarians usually argued for brutal slum clearances and the expulsion of workers from the central districts of cities, an example of which took place in Paris during the infamous urban reforms Baron Haussmann carried out in the mid-nineteenth century (Taunton 2009). In other cases, the contribution of progressive sanitarian hygienists such as Rudolf Virchow constructed the discursive basis for later municipal efforts to reform public housing or the establishment of construction regulations and city planning. Certainly, the sanitary movement was highly successful in instilling a specific disgust for 'filth' in urban populations of all classes while also propagating new daily practices for washing bodies, homes, and clothes, among others (Cleere 2016; Melosi 2000).

Secondly, in regarding miasmas as the main cause of disease, members of the sanitarian movement believed that ensuring the constant circulation of air and water in cities was crucial to prevent the outbreak of epidemics. In fact, if miasma emanated from decaying organic matter, flowing water was an effective means to quickly drive dangerous substances away from cities before they began to decompose. The attraction to the idea of circulation propagated by the sanitarians was connected to both the rise of liberalism and free market theories, based on the free circulation of capital and goods as well as the medical principles concerning arteriovenous circulation in the human body (Joyce 2003). Sanitarians often proposed analogies between the city and the body, especially when the concept of circulation was concerned. Similar to the arteries carrying oxygenated blood to the body's organs, flowing fresh water had to be brought into private homes and, once it had been used to wash or to flush away debris and excrement, it had to enter – analogously to the venous system – another flowing system to carry it away from the city. The dirty water flow had to run underground so as to prevent any air contamination from taking place

(Gandy 2014). Furthermore, streets needed to be paved and regularly cleaned in order to avert the accumulation of liquids or any kind of emanation from the soil that could reach the air. The reduced population density and the construction of wide streets and parks would also ensure the constant circulation of air so that winds could remove miasma easily if they were to accumulate.

Even after the beginning of the slow decline in the miasmatic theories on which the sanitary movement mainly rested and the rise of germ theory in the late nineteenth century, the aforementioned principles established by the sanitary movement largely remained valid. In general, the sanitary movement has had an almost incalculable impact on the ways in which both public and private spaces in cities have been perceived and constructed from the nineteenth century until today. Moreover, even though the leading figures of the movement mostly emerged in Europe, its influence went well beyond the boundaries of the European continent. Together with epidemic diseases, sanitary theories travelled easily between the European and the American continents, which from the mid-nineteenth century were increasingly connected through a regular traffic of steamships. The postcolonial nations on the American continent were deeply influenced by the contributions of European hygienists while also consistently providing a key contribution to the global debate on the sanitisation of cities (Armus and López Denis 2011; Birn 2018; Ramsden 2018).

Similarly, cities ruled by European empires were decidedly under the influence of the sanitary movement, yet they also deeply shaped both the rise and the form of ideas about santitation. In fact, perhaps the most relevant novelty in nineteenth-century city planning introduced by the sanitary movement rested on the biopolitical regulation of urban populations (Baldwin 1999; Foucault 2007). A colonial medical analysis of the problems posed by the settling of Europeans in colonial regions, and the feeling that urban space in the colonies was more malleable than in Europe, were possibly the primary motors behind the very idea that epidemics could be prevented by intervening to change urban space and the practices of urbanites. Certainly by the second half of the nineteenth century, metropolitan and colonial urban centres were the objects of hygienic experiments, most notably carried out under the principles of the sanitary movement. The knowledge gathered through these experiments moved back and forth across the globe, transported by the medical, military, and administrative personnel of imperial governments (Harrison 2010).

1.5 Colonialism, Warm Climates, and Tropical Medicine

In the centuries spanning the European conquest of the Americas in the sixteenth century and the emergence of vast overland colonies in large parts of Asia and Africa in the nineteenth century, medicine featured as a central ally and resource of empire-building. European physicians were on the front line – at the beginning more modestly and later with greater success – in decreasing mortality rates among colonial explorers, armies, officials, and settlers. Furthermore, medical knowledge became an integral part of colonisers' attempts to gain control of colonised populations, during which Western medicine was often offered as a demonstration of an allegedly benevolent superiority. In contrast, medicine was not only a tool of empire but was itself formed through colonial experiences. Contact with new diseases, medical observations allowed by long maritime travel, the exchange of knowledge with indigenous populations, and the resulting acquisition of new drugs and ingredients all contributed to the development of modern Western medicine. The very possibility that Western medicine can be regarded as a universal doctrine conceivably derives from its character as a construct mediated through centuries of global hybridisation (Chakrabarti 2014). A classic example of this process of hybridisation is provided by the history of the cinchona, a tree native to Peru and known among South American indigenous populations as a remedy for fever. In the seventeenth century, instructed by Native American healers, priests of the Society of Jesus transferred this knowledge to Europe, where they experimented with cinchona in treatments for malaria, a disease unknown in the Americas before the European invasions. During the nineteenth century, the active ingredient of the cinchona tree was identified as quinine, which became the basis of the modern malaria treatment and prophylaxis adopted in many regions of the world from the early twentieth century onwards (Packard 2007).

Parallel to the expansion of colonialism, a specific area of medicine emerged during the nineteenth century that became known as 'tropical medicine'. Highlighting the exceptional position occupied by colonies, tropical medicine is the only medical branch defined through a specific geographic and climatic area, in this case the tropics. The discipline originally rested on the presumed distinction between the diseases in the tropics and those of the temperate zones. In reality, many so-called tropical diseases, which may have become less common in temperate areas, are not necessarily confined to the tropics and are instead mostly 'diseases of poverty, social deprivation, malnutrition, and insanitary conditions' (Arnold 1996, 4). Malaria, for instance, the most prominent among the tropical diseases, was indeed constantly present in the temperate regions of the Mediterranean and ravaged generations of Southern Europeans, as highlighted by the eradication efforts that lasted in Italy until the 1960s (Snowden 2006).

The status of tropical disease within Western medicine is intimately linked to the exceptional position the tropics have come to occupy in the colonial imagination. Alternatively described as paradise or hell, the tropics have played a physical and conceptual role throughout the history of colonialism that has been permeated by a sense of 'otherness' vis-à-vis Europe (Cagle 2018). Since the accounts of Christopher Columbus on the island of Hispaniola, the tropics, with their supposedly exotic fauna, flora, and climate, have been described as a web of fascination and repulsion. If the register of the paradisiac prevailed in Columbus's description, other colonial descriptions often underlined the pestilential and threatening dimension of the tropics, which made them appear as the 'white man's grave' (Curtin 1990, 1989). From this unique stance on the tropics, physicians focusing on warm climates often considered diseases in the tropics to be more violent and more rapidly spread than in temperate regions, a conviction that often served also to justify more brutal and hasty solutions than in temperate regions.

As physicians largely conceived epidemic disease as the result of miasmas emanating from cadavers and swamps, the humid and stultifying heat associated with tropical climates and the rapid pace with which putrefaction could occur aroused a construction of the tropics as intrinsically unhealthy environments. The higher incidence of certain epidemic diseases such as yellow fever was therefore connected with the idea that tropical environments were full of miasmas and inherently insalubrious. Furthermore, physicians educated in the humoral tradition generally considered warmth and humidity especially harmful for European individuals, whose constitutions and temperaments were supposedly not able to acclimate to the tropics. The poor resistance of the European constitution in warm climates was considered among the main reasons for the different rates of mortality between indigenous populations and Europeans until the end of the nineteenth century (Arnold 1996). Together with the assumption that contrasting climates engendered contrasting diseases, tropical medicine revolved around the notion that humans possess different grades of resistance to disease based on their constitution, which was often connected to notions on race. On one hand, the grade of acclimation – the amount of time European settlers had spent in a certain place – was considered pivotal in determining their resistance to disease. On the other hand, giving rise to racial explanations of disease, the allegedly different bodily constitution of Europeans was held responsible for their higher death rates in the tropics. From this racial assumption, tropical medicine developed as a discipline that theorised a wealth of racial biological differences between human beings (Harrison 1999, 9).

These notions had remarkable influences on cities worldwide and served as one of the main 'scientific' foundations behind practices of urban segregation on a racial basis (Anderson 2006, 1996; Chalhoub 1993). Resembling the treatment reserved for the urban working classes in Europe, the indigenous population was held accountable for the moral decay and filth that caused epidemics in the colonial context. In the colonies, however, the indigenous populations, which in many cases had been in contact with diseases such as malaria and yellow fever from their infancy, seemed less affected by these diseases than the European settlers, giving rise to even more radical sentiments of suspicion among their colonisers. What is more, if projects of urban segregation on a class basis in Europe often failed under the pressure of the rising political and symbolic power of the white working classes, in the colonies, urban segregation was carried out by military force with the engagement of imperial governments. Throughout the nineteenth century, using the knowledge produced by tropical medicine, colonial regimes attempted to apply the system of segregating European settlers from indigenous populations in vast parts of the American continent, Asia, and Africa (Nightingale 2012).

In addition to segregation, tropical medicine and other connected theories, which saw miasmas rising from the soil and decomposing matter as responsible for disease, generally served as the groundwork for urban planning in European colonies. The principles concerning racial segregation and soil analyses, ventilation, and temperature were pivotal in determining both the choice of particular locations and the way in which the urban living quarters of colonisers were built. For instance, in India, British officials not only seasonally retired to 'hill stations', but also often constructed their houses on stilts so as to elevate them from the ground and protect them from the allegedly poisonous emanations from the soil. Merging the principle of the hill station with racial segregation, the colonial government of British India developed a system of so-called cantonments in the 1860s – military camps located 'away from the noxious odours of the "native" population, preferably to windward' (Curtin 1985, 595). Originally developed for the military, this principle soon became the principal pattern in the construction of residential districts for civilian settlers. Even beyond the British empire and in non-tropical colonial regions such as French Algeria, 'tropical' principles were applied to architecture and urban planning. With a climate very much resembling that of southern France, Algeria underlines the fact that the adjective 'tropical' was rather a synonym for 'colonial' and that 'tropical' medicine was a branch of medicine that did not necessarily focus on tropical climates but rather on the health of European settlers (Osborne 1996).

1.6 The Germ Theory of Disease

Historiography has often been inclined to describe the emergence of the germ theory of disease as a sensational discovery and a sudden earthquake that shook the very foundations of medicine as it had been known until the late 1870s. In fact, though it had been preceded by several scholars theorising upon it, tangible proof that epidemic diseases were caused by microorganisms indeed proved somewhat revolutionary. However, it can be argued that it was precisely due to its revolutionary character that germ theory entered only slowly into the canon of medicine. Narrations concerning the rise of germ theory often concentrate on two scientists – the chemist Louis Pasteur and the physician Robert Koch – dominating centre stage as the heroes of microbiology. Similarly to the idea of the sudden revolution in medicine, the heroic narratives of Pasteur and Koch have largely been debunked in recent decades and substituted by a consideration of the long institutional, technical, and cultural series of prerequisites from which the two scientists benefitted (Latour 1988). The improvement of the optical microscope, to name just one of these prerequisites, was pivotal in the rise of microbiology and, for instance, viruses, which cannot be seen through optical devices, could be identified only in the 1930s, when electronic micro-scopes became available (Ruestow 1996).

Pasteur and Koch were the inventors neither of concepts such as contagion, which had a long-standing tradition in religious thinking, nor the existence of microscopic animalcules or germs. Nevertheless, they were certainly protagon-ists of a new shift in medical epistemology; the laboratory and not the hospital ward alone was to be the new locus in which 'scientific' medical knowledge was produced. By cultivating bacteria in his laboratory with the help of his micro-scope, Pasteur could demonstrate that the spoilage of milk and wine, which he deemed similar to processes of putrefaction, depended on the action of micro-organisms. He proved it is possible to destroy bacteria through heat and prevent food from spoiling, laying the foundation for a process – named 'pasteurisa-tion' – that prevented micro-organic contamination in milk and other foods. Furthermore, Pasteur explored the implication of these discoveries in wound infection and disease and speculated that all diseases may have their cause in microscopic germs. Expanding on his theory, he also experimented with methods to attenuate the virulence of microorganisms and thus delivered initial explanations on the working mechanism of vaccines (Gaynes 2011). In fact, in the specific case of smallpox, vaccination had been practised since the turn of the nineteenth century but without clarifications on how it functioned (Bazin 2000). Koch is often referred to as the co-founder of the germ theory of disease. Introducing significant innovations concerning the microscope and the visual-isation of transparent bacteria through dying solutions, in 1882, Koch was able to isolate and demonstrate that *Mycobacterium tuberculosis* was the cause of tuberculosis, thus shedding light on a major disease whose causation was hitherto shrouded in mystery (Brock 1999).

The competition between European empires at the end of the nineteenth century contributed to the transformation of the two scientists into heroic champions for their respective countries, Louis Pasteur for the French empire and Robert Koch for the German empire. Their achievements were heralded as demonstrations of superiority over other nations and empires as well as the colonies. In fact, since John Snow and Filippo Pacini's respective mid-nineteenth-century publications concerning the waterborne nature of cholera and the identification of the microorganism had gone unnoticed, the discovery of the bacteria responsible for cholera was a much-sought-after international goal that spurred inter-imperial competition. In this atmosphere, as cholera broke out in Egypt in 1883, the French, Belgian, and German empires sent delegations to identify the microorganism responsible for the epidemic. The head of the French delegation succumbed to cholera and Koch's team soon left Egypt, where the epidemic was faltering, and headed to India. There they were eventually able to identify the *Vibrio cholerae* as the bacteria responsible for the disease and were received in Berlin as heroes (Watts 1999). Confirming the model of the imperial research team sent into the colonies to identify microorganisms responsible for disease, in Hong Kong in 1894, the Japanese physician Kitasato Shibasaburo, and soon after the Frenchman Alexandre Yersin, isolated *Yersinia pestis*, the bacteria responsible for bubonic plague (Snowden 2019). If the outcomes of these discoveries were enormous in terms of imperial propaganda, they initially failed to lead to effective treatments for diseases caused by microorganisms. The substances that can destroy bacteria inside the human body – antibiotics – were developed in the 1930s and largely used only after the Second World War. Therefore, lacking the means to treat diseases while they were discovering their causes, physicians educated in germ theory focused on disease prevention. Pasteurisation and antiseptic practices, procedures that destroyed microorganisms outside the human body, constituted great successes connected with germ theory that consistently contributed to the prevention of epidemic diseases.

In the context of urban hygiene, the findings of germ theory were slowly integrated and superimposed onto the principles of miasmatism established by the sanitary movement. Germ theory added new aspects and stresses to the principles preached by the sanitarians. For instance, retaining the centrality of water supply and sewer systems to avoid waterborne diseases such as cholera, germ theory stressed water filtration to eliminate microorganisms: when Hamburg was hit by a major cholera epidemic in 1892, hygienists educated in germ theory insisted that the water infrastructure was not sufficient as it lacked water filtration (Evans 1987). Until the first decades of the twentieth century, miasmatic and germ-based aetiologies – that is, explanations of the causes of disease – were often presented as entwined. For instance, after the identification of *Yersinia pestis*, the aetiology of bubonic plague, a disease that in most cases does not spread through direct human contact but through fleas, remained a mystery (Echenberg 2007). Consequently, in establishing measures to prevent outbreaks of bubonic plague, the lessons from germ theory were overlaid onto those of the sanitary movement, a phenomenon that also occurred for other diseases and especially in tropical colonies, where miasmas were deemed especially dangerous (Curtin 1985).

If the principles of urban planning and infrastructure construction based on germ theory did not initially diverge greatly from those of the sanitary movement, the two schools had rather contrasting opinions on the everyday practices of urban dwellers. Indeed, the idea 'that microscopic living particles were the agents of contagion, that sick bodies shed germs into the environment, and that disease spread by seemingly innocuous behaviours such as coughing, sneezing and spitting, sharing common drinking cups, or failing to wash hands before eating' radically changed the life of urbanites (Tomes 1999, 7). Especially the germ-theory-based 'war on tuberculosis' had a wide range of outcomes. Looking at fashion, for instance, if having a beard was almost compulsory for European bourgeois men in the second half of the nineteenth century, the idea that facial hair could harbour microorganisms and especially the feared *Mycobacterium tuberculosis* prompted a progressive shift towards shaved facial hair. For middle- and upper-class women, germs were among the main preoccupations behind the decline of skirts with long trains and full-skirted fashion in general, which had all but disappeared from their wardrobes by the turn of the twentieth century. Germ theory also inspired the creation of antiseptic concepts in decoration and housekeeping, which had a specific gender focus on women and pointed to the recruitment of mostly working- and middle-class mothers as the agents in tuberculosis prevention in private homes (Tomes 1999). Furthermore, hitherto common behaviours, such as spitting on public transportation, were forbidden and severely stigmatised.

The idea that diseases were caused by close contact with other human beings who could carry infectious microorganisms greatly contributed to the proliferation of a certain suspicion towards practices of dense urban living. In the context of the war on tuberculosis, the stress of germ-theory-inspired hygienists on outdoor life in 'unspoiled nature' as both prevention and treatment of the disease inspired a negative image of the city. Germ theory and the war on tuberculosis did not invent anti-urban sentiments, yet they certainly contributed to the creation of a discourse concerning the perilous nature of cities. In this sense, germ theory certainly contributed to an increase in the phenomena of middle- and upper-class urban flight and patterns of suburbanisation in its application in the war on tuberculosis. In some cases, such as in the United States, suburbanisation and racial segregation overlapped as germ theory merged with ideas concerning tropical medicine and different human constitutions based on race (Roberts 2009).

2 Cholera

Cholera was not the most dramatic epidemic disease in terms of lives lost, yet it may have been the most feared of the long nineteenth century. The reasons for its terrorising character can firstly be found in its specific characteristic as an infection that can suddenly appear and quickly kill a great number of people. The disease spread through the faecal-oral route via both direct contact and the contamination of water and food. Especially in the case of contaminated drinking water in cities, cholera could promptly infect thousands of people, giving rise to a feeling of a mass poisoning. Secondly, cultural and aesthetic ideas contributed to cholera's reputation as a truly gruesome event. In fact, the faecal character of cholera, which mainly manifests itself as violent diarrhoea, was deemed utterly shameful, dehumanising, and indecent. The severe diarrhoea-induced dehydration caused in patients a state of delirium, unquenchable thirst, and a bluish hue of the skin, all symptoms that transformed humans into ghastly shadows. What is more, imbued with Orientalist and racist fantasies, nineteenth-century Europeans perceived cholera as a racialised intruder from the East, originating as it did from India and accordingly earning the name 'Asiatic cholera'. Finally, although cholera was endemic in Bengal, it was a novelty outside of the region and, after 1817, the disease spread at alarming speed. In seven subsequent pandemics, cholera reached nearly all corners of the world, some repeatedly. Cholera pandemics typically lasted from one to two decades and came in short succession: the first pandemic lasted circa 1817–24, the second circa 1826–37, the third circa 1846–62, the fourth circa 1863–75, the fifth circa 1881–96, and the sixth circa 1899–1923. A seventh pandemic, mainly caused by a new and milder strain of the bacteria called *El Tor*, began in 1961 and has not yet been eradicated, resulting in occasional but nonetheless dramatic outbreaks.

Apart from the great fear that cholera caused among contemporaries, the disease has also drawn the interest of numerous historians. They have often considered cholera as a phenomenon that can encapsulate certain central features and contradictions of the nineteenth century with great clarity. For instance, the spread of cholera beyond Bengal is embedded in the transportation revolution and the dramatically increasing capacity of the movement of people and goods across the globe. Steam navigation, railroads and trains, and the construction of canals, most notably the Suez Canal, enhanced the pace and quantity of travel, allowing cholera to spread virulently into different regions. The worldwide expansion of European empires also played a major role in the diffusion of the disease. A key tenet of nineteenth-century history, imperialist ambitions lay behind the motive for British troop movements in India, which were among the main causes for the spread of the disease outside the Asian subcontinent. The rapid means of maritime and terrestrial transportation could then carry the disease across the globe and from the colonies back into the imperial metropoles and beyond (Hamlin 2009).

Cholera is not only intrinsically connected to the deployment of pivotal nineteenth-century processes such as imperialism and the transportation revolution, but it has also been considered by historians as a means to highlight certain contradictions that defined the century. For instance, cholera questioned liberalism, another major nineteenth-century 'ism', and intersected problematically with one of its main tenets – the idea that the free movement of goods, ideas, capital, and to a certain extent of people, was synonymous with progress. Indeed, cholera was a thorn in the side of liberal ideas and practices of free trade and the movement of goods. The hegemony of miasmatic assertions, insisting that locally accumulated 'filth' was the main origin of the disease, endured until the end of the century and integrated with other aetiological notions, which considered the movement of people and goods as a further reason for the spread of disease (Harrison 2012). Interweaving notions of miasma and contagion, governments worldwide implemented regimes of surveillance, coercion, and quarantine that strongly limited freedom of movement and sought to implement strict restrictions on people and goods in circulation. In fact, the limitations on movement, which were paradoxically justified through the need to defend the safety of the regime of free trade, mostly affected specific groups of people who were deemed especially likely to carry and spread the disease.

Undermining universalist claims of liberalism, the identification and stigmatisation of supposedly dangerous groups was intimately connected with questions of race, ethnicity, religion, class, and gender. For instance, the strictest limitations of movement were imposed on Muslim pilgrims travelling from South and Southeast Asia to Mecca (Huber 2013; Tagliacozzo 2013). In the eyes of the European imperial powers, the circulation of goods clearly took precedence over the movement of people for religious purposes, which were instead object of restrictions. These limitations were legitimised by the rationale of protecting the free circulation of other more important individuals and goods. The repressive limitation of the Muslim pilgrims also prompted some of the first experiments in international cooperation. Surveillance on the movement of people in western Asia and the Eastern Mediterranean required far-reaching collaboration between different nations and empires. When it came to cholera and the damages it caused to the circulation of goods, at the height of the age of imperialism, empires and nations were able to temporarily suspend the competition between them and to find solutions to the otherwise diverse and potentially conflicting requirements of maritime quarantine. Held between 1851 and 1894, international sanitary conferences on cholera reinforced the imperial world order on one hand, as a small number of representatives from a handful of European nations and empires took decisions for the whole globe, while, on the other, they also lay the groundwork for future internationalist projects (Huber 2020; Zeheter 2016).

The challenge to liberalism in the form of cholera not only affected international trade, but also questioned its tenets at both the urban and regional levels. In the case of cities in Europe and on the American continent, where population growth and the weakening of ancien-régime communitarianism were enhancing urban anonymity and individual freedom, cholera also questioned another central tenet of liberalism, namely individualism. In fact, despite the increased familiarity with the disease in the nineteenth century, medical experts would often attribute the spread of cholera to the failings of single individuals, especially those of 'libertines' indulging in eating, drinking, and sexual excesses. They were deemed responsible for creating a condition of physical weakness that rendered them susceptible to cholera, which in turn enabled the disease to spread through their weak bodies to the rest of the community. Therefore, cholera often inspired moralising campaigns that underlined the need for individual behaviour to be attuned to the needs of the whole community. Since infection rates were generally higher in poor neighbourhoods, the attention of experts and leaders mostly focused on these living spaces. The moral principles to follow were those of the ruling classes, while the working classes or other rather marginalised groups were often targeted with repressive campaigns. The measures to clean living quarters and moralise the behaviour of workers and marginalised groups were often brutal and met fierce resistance. However, discussions on the measures adopted to prevent the spread of cholera among the urban working classes were not exclusively repressive and also encouraged greater awareness among politicians and the upper classes of the living conditions of the poor. Urban discussions on the prevention of epidemics, most notably cholera, often inspired both philanthropic actions and reformist endeavours that laid the groundwork for later contestations of the urban status quo (Evans 1987; Hamlin 1998).

However, the somewhat reformist and progressive aspects of the discussions on cholera applied almost solely to cities in Europe and on the American continent. The situation differed in part in cities under colonial rule, where imperial governments were generally less engaged in preventing disease in the whole population. The measures expounded by the sanitarian movement included the construction of costly and complex urban infrastructure, especially concerning water provision and sewer systems, that often proved beyond empires' financial resources. Though the matter was tackled rather contrastingly during various periods of the nineteenth century and in different locations, the focus of colonial administration was usually placed on preventing settlers, colonial armies, imperial agents, and colonial elites from falling sick (Harrison 2018). Furthermore, colonial rulers tended to consider cholera as an endemic and unsolvable issue facing indigenous populations. The main goal of colonial administrations was centred on keeping the disease out of their cantonments, while efforts concerning city planning and sanitarian reform mostly focused on the neighbourhoods and areas in which colonial elites resided (Arnold 1993).

2.1 Paris: Cholera, Fear, and Revolution

During the second cholera pandemic from circa 1826 to 1837, the disease achieved a new geographic expansion, reaching Europe, North Africa, and North America. The disease affected two of the most populous cities of the period for the first time in 1832, Paris and London. The arrival of cholera in the British and the French capitals and in Europe in general has often been associated with two main keywords: fear and revolution. In terms of fear, the failure of both medicine and government in the case of Paris became dramatically apparent and resulted in widespread panic when circa 20,000 of the city's 650,000 inhabitants, or approximately 3 per cent of the urban population, rapidly succumbed to cholera. Hitherto considered the pinnacle of European medical science, Parisian medicine proved helpless and failed completely to prevent the spread of the disease and to find a cure for it. This failure was especially strongly felt because it came as a surprise, as Paris and France had previously been spared from major epidemics for an extended period of time.

When cholera hit Paris, France was far from free of disease. Since the end of the second plague pandemic, which had hit Marseilles one last time in 1720, the country had been the victim of several epidemics but none of an emotional magnitude comparable with the plague. The latest great epidemics had broken out in the army at a sizeable distance from mainland France, most notably during Napoleon's campaigns in Haiti and Russia. The military contingent, which Napoleon had sent in 1802 to restore colonial rule and slavery in Haiti, returned to France defeated and decimated by yellow fever (McNeill 2010). Similarly, the invasion of Russia in 1812 ended with the dramatic retreat of Napoleon's Grande Armée, which had been recurringly ravaged by dysentery and typhus (Talty 2009). Against this backdrop, before cholera broke out in 1832, Parisians and especially bourgeois elements had come to consider extremely deadly epidemics as more of a problem for the army and the colonies. Furthermore, due to developments in the techniques of inoculation and vaccination, even smallpox, a highly contagious and often fatal disease, seemed far less threatening in the 1830s than previously. As a disease deemed indecent and 'uncivilised', cholera unexpectedly challenged the self-confident attitude of the ruling bourgeois who believed that the degree of 'civilisation' attained by France and its capital city would be able to fend off the 'barbaric' cholera (Delaporte 1986).

Notwithstanding the confidence affluent Parisians exuded at the beginning of the 1830s, Paris was an unhealthy city of dramatic contrasts, as it had been for most of its history. A feature that still characterises Paris today, the coexistence of multiple functions made the city a showcase for the French monarchy and aristocracy as well as a scholarly, commercial, and productive hub. Consequently, monarchs, aristocrats, and high-ranking clerics lived in direct proximity with merchants, artisans, and workers. For centuries, the growth of Paris was the result of stratified and uncontrolled building practices only partially countered by the more easily governable properties of the crown and religious institutions. This long tradition of relatively spontaneous growth first came to a halt in 1783–4 as a set of royal regulations was passed requiring property owners to submit construction plans to the administration for approval. This was a novelty that pointed towards bringing the bulk of construction works under the control of public authorities and laid the groundwork for successive attempts to plan urban space, with more than the usual focus on the great projects of monarchs. This set of new regulations was approved only five years before the outbreak of the French Revolution, an event which led to a series of key changes in the urban landscape of Paris. The plans of the revolutionary administrations mostly focused on the construction of a network of straight and wide streets connecting and enhancing the aesthetic grandeur of the city's most important public buildings.

The principles laid out in the revolutionary years, which were later reinterpreted as essential for the enhancement of circulation and the ability for fast transport through the city, played an influential role in successive projects and represented the ideological blueprint of the reforms realised during the nineteenth century, most notably by Baron Haussmann. The destruction of the bulky Bastille, for instance, eventually facilitated plans for the construction of an east–west thoroughfare on the northern bank of the Seine. Furthermore, the massive confiscation of aristocratic and ecclesiastic properties and the breaching of the city walls allowed for further speculative expansion of Paris beyond its dense and ancient city centre around the Île de la Cité. However, if the successive revolutionary administrations that rapidly followed one another were keen to make major plans for the capital city, their actual outcome on built space, especially in the context of the old city, was rather modest. In fact, although the revolutionaries had been successful in confiscating land previously in the hands of aristocrats and religious orders in the immediate surroundings of the city, their impact on the highly complex palimpsest of construction and property rights in the old city was much more limited.

Even the authoritarian Napoleon, while building certain projects planned during the revolution such as the east–west thoroughfare, was virtually unable to bring about major changes in the old city. His lasting legacy on Paris rather consisted of a reorientation of the city towards the west; after connecting the Louvre with the Tuileries and the Champs-Élysées, his interventions paved the way for the expansion of affluent neighbourhoods to the west of the city, away from the winding streets of the old city. Therefore, notwithstanding the changes carried out during the revolution and the Napoleonic era, as the Bourbon monarchs were restored to the French throne in 1814–15, the Parisian old city surrounding the Île de la Cité was utterly congested, had virtually no access to sewers, and had a poor fresh water supply. Simultaneously, a new belt of affluent neighbourhoods in the west and poorer mixed-function areas in the other areas, such as the famously riotous Faubourg Saint-Antoine, were growing substantially (Jordan 1995, 13–40).

The beliefs of affluent Parisians aside, on the eve of the cholera epidemic in 1832, Paris and especially its poorly serviced central and eastern neighbourhoods were inadequately prepared to face a major epidemic. Authorities were partially aware of this and, while expressing confidence that a civilised city would be spared barbaric disease such as cholera, they began preparing as the epidemic spread across Europe. In fact, cholera had arrived in Moscow in September 1830 and in Poland in April 1831. In October of the same year, it reached Hamburg. It eventually reached London in February 1832 (Bourdelais and Raulot 1987). While the disease made headway in Western Europe, Parisian authorities put initial measures in place to assess the sanitary situation of the city. A series of neighbourhood commissions were entrusted with the task of exploring different urban areas to find insanitary conditions, such as stagnant water, overcrowding, and the presence of decomposing matter. The results heightened authorities' suspicion that insalubrious conditions were ubiquitous and that an attempt to remove them would imply a long-term engagement to reconstruct a whole part of the city. Conscious that the urban fabric could not be changed in weeks or even months, Parisian authorities focused on more inconspicuous interventions. A clear example was a mandate to reduce population density in the poorer neighbourhoods by forcing vagabonds and seasonal workers to return to their provinces of origin. This mandate would have required an enormous deployment of police and was not actually enforceable, but it clearly expresses the Parisian authorities' belief that the poor and their lodgings were the cause of the spread of cholera.

When the epidemic broke out in the spring of 1832, the authorities followed the traditional guidelines adopted in previous epidemics – ordering a general clean-up of urban space, hospitalising and isolating the sick, and organising charity donations for the poor, who were disproportionally affected by cholera. The church and the crown were on the front line in administering charity organisations and hospitals. However, if during previous epidemics both institutions had enjoyed widespread approval among the underprivileged classes, this was no longer the case in 1832. The revolutionary experiences of the previous decades had deeply undermined the trust the crown and the church traditionally enjoyed among the popular classes. Beneficiaries were generally unsatisfied with donations, which came with their own humiliating rules and logic. Furthermore, forced hospitalisations were perceived as inhuman and, for all intents and purposes, a death sentence to serve without the comfort of the family. On the other end of the social spectrum, the wealthy believed the poor classes and their alleged filthiness, debauchery, and intemperance were responsible for the spread of cholera into their ranks. As a consequence, while cholera was already causing hundreds of deaths per day in April 1832, the authorities strengthened surveillance on the behaviour and living conditions of the poorer classes and their compliance with sanitary regulations. The surveillance system was centred on neighbourhood commissions, often guided by physicians assigned the task of making house calls, punishing unhygienic behaviour, identifying and hospitalising the sick, and organising the speedy removal of corpses.

Disproportionally affecting poorer Parisians and derived from the general distrust espoused by the bourgeois for the working classes, this set of measures met fierce opposition from the Parisian lower classes. In addition to protests against the repressive measure against them, many underprivileged Parisians interpreted the fact that cholera almost solely affected them as a clue that the rich had decided to eliminate a part of the city's population. The sudden onset of the symptoms of cholera and its progress contributed to the impression that the sick had been poisoned. Targets of the anger of poorer Parisians were initially physicians, who were largely considered agents of the bourgeoisie sent to poison fountains and wells. As Malthusian discourses connecting figures in population growth with the availability of resources began to circulate in France, cholera rioters accused the ruling bourgeois class of being at the head of a conspiracy to solve the problem of the ratio between resources and population by killing as many poor Parisians as possible (Delaporte 1986; Chevalier 1973; Kudlick 1996).

Dramatic cholera riots such as those that took place in Paris in 1832 also occurred in many other European countries, including England, Russia, and Italy. Questions on the context of these riots in the wider framework of the age of revolution have been at the forefront of the historiography on cholera; for instance, historians have wondered if the cholera riots were mere localised and short-lived outbursts of violence or noteworthy revolutionary moments in which generalised political and social claims were articulated and major revolutions prepared. Answers to these questions can hardly be univocal and depend greatly on the specific regional and political contexts in which cholera riots developed and occurred (Cohn 2018). However, in the Parisian case, the specific chronology of cholera epidemics seems to point to the fact that cholera was more a consequence than a cause of major revolutions. The epidemic of 1832 occurred just two years after the July Revolution of 1830 that had decreed the end of the Bourbon Restoration and the beginning of the monarchy of Louis Philippe I, otherwise called the Bourgeois Monarch, underlining his political alignment with the growing bourgeois class. Making its second appearance in the city in 1849, cholera also directly followed the revolution of 1848 that had concluded Louis Philippe's reign and inaugurated the Second Republic, which came to an end three years later with the coronation of Emperor Napoleon III (Evans 1988; Kudlick 1996).

Despite being more of a consequence than a cause of revolution, the cholera riots in Paris gave rise to particularly relevant patterns of new political and social antagonism which intensified in the following decades. In contrast to popular protests that often accompanied the outbreak of the plague in early modern Europe, usually targeting the Jewish population and other minorities, cholera fuelled class riots in the 1830s. Cholera is not the reason for the emergence of modern notions and practices of class. However, the riots of 1832 were one of the first occasions in which working classes, partially in alliance with urban middle classes, were clearly pitted against the richer bourgeoisie. Unlike the French Revolution and the July Revolution of 1830, in which workers and the bourgeoisie fought side by side in overthrowing the *ancien régime*, the cholera riots showed that this anti-aristocratic alliance was built on a rather fragile basis, particularly as the Parisian bourgeoisie increasingly became the city's new powerhouse. It is certainly not by chance that, shortly after proclaiming himself emperor of the French, Napoleon III appointed Georges-Eugène Haussmann as prefect of Paris in 1853 and entrusted him to usher in a radical reconfiguration of the city. Napoleon III and Baron

Haussmann had in mind for Paris a new type of city that would be rid of two key problems: epidemic disease, eminently cholera, and revolution (Jordan 1995; Kirkland 2013).

2.2 Buenos Aires: Discussing Industry and Models of Urban Modernity

Spanish settlers founded the port city of Buenos Aires in the sixteenth century a few kilometres south of the confluence of the Paraná and Uruguay Rivers, forming the Río de la Plata, or River Plate. In its first two centuries of existence, Buenos Aires developed into somewhat of a backwater commercial centre of the Spanish empire. Merchants from Buenos Aires initially smuggled silver and slaves, slipping into the grey areas between several Atlantic imperial powers, and gradually specialised in the more legitimate export of leather and cowhides. The city was, in fact, not only strategically positioned on the fluvial connection between the Paraná basin and the Atlantic, but also the main urban centre of the pampas, a vast prairie region that developed into a site of extensive cattle production from the seventeenth century onwards. If the exploitation of this animal resource, richly present in the grasslands surrounding the city, mostly took place in the open countryside, the situation had changed considerably by the early nineteenth century. Following its de facto independence from Spain in 1810, Buenos Aires progressively transformed into an international centre of a new type of industry of cattle transformation based on the processing of meat and cowhide through salting and drying. From 1810 until the 1860s, the industry of the *saladeros*, as the meat-salting factories of Buenos Aires were called, flourished, delivering the lion's share of the city's trade and of Argentina as a whole, exporting mainly jerked beef, cowhides, and tallow to Brazil, Cuba, and several European countries. The *saladeros* also employed a major part of the city's working population, which consisted more and more of migrants of European descent from the mid-nineteenth century onwards (Carbone 2022a, 2022b; Sluyter 2010).

When cholera reached Buenos Aires for the first time in 1867 during the fourth pandemic, the presence of these industries discharging their organic waste from the cattle-slaughtering process into the Riachuelo, a small slow-moving tributary of the River Plate, became a source of great controversy. Indeed, not only the living conditions and behaviour of the poor but also, in conjunction with the teachings of miasmatic theory, emissions from the decomposition of organic matter and foul odours in general were viewed as possible factors at the root of epidemics. The considerable quantity of organic waste the *saladeros* produced often provoked 'great stink' crises similar to those that affected London in 1858 and Paris in the 1880s and 1890s (Barnes 2006; Halliday 2001). In spite of the fact that the debate on the legitimacy of the pollution created by the meat-salting industries had re-emerged on each occasion that a 'foul smelling' crisis occurred from the early 1850s onwards, the outbreak of cholera in 1867 gave far greater urgency and weight to this discussion. The disease appeared in the last months of 1867 and peaked again at the end of 1868; it did not disappear completely until 1869. During this time, cholera killed 5,000 people, almost 3 per cent of the whole urban population of approximately 180,000 inhabitants (Fiquepron 2020). Although most fatalities were among the ranks of the city's poorer workers, cholera also struck the upper classes, increasing the urgency to resolve the problem of the 'odorous' Riachuelo. If the outbreak of cholera bestowed greater significance on the discussions concerning the meat-salting industries, it was in fact an epidemic of yellow fever that brought the lengthy debate to its conclusion. When yellow fever broke out in 1871, causing an even greater catastrophe than cholera and killing approximately 14,000 *porteños* – as the inhabitants of Buenos Aires are called – a parliamentary session decreed a permanent ban on the *saladeros* from their original location on the southern outskirts of the city.

Triggered by the outbreak of the cholera epidemic, the discussions on the *saladeros* were not only a debate on the factories themselves; they soon developed into a general debate on industry, urban modernity, and the future of Buenos Aires as a whole. In discussions in several media outlets and institutions between 1867 and 1871, *porteño* elites were divided into two opposing parties concerning the '*saladero* question'. On one hand was a wide group of journalists and politicians, who, suspecting a connection with cholera and yellow fever, denounced the pollution caused by the meat-salting factories and questioned the general legitimacy of industry to operate in the immediate vicinity of the city. They described the *saladeros* as a symbol of backwardness and saw a direct link between the barbaric practices that allegedly took place in these factories with the barbarism they ascribed to cholera. On the other hand, another group of journalists, politicians, and technicians argued in favour of the *saladeros* and advocated for their continued presence in the city. They envisioned the *saladeros* as a modern and indispensable branch of industry for Buenos Aires to remain on a path of modernity. Though they may have had alternative viewpoints on the issue of the meat-salting factories, the two parties shared a common frame of reference – the experiences of other cities, mainly in Western Europe, concerning the issue of industrial pollution and its correlation with epidemics.[1]

---

[1] Information contained in these sections is based on my own research on documents, newspapers, reports, and publications of the period. More comprehensive versions of the arguments presented and of the sources analysed are contained in (Carbone 2022a, 2022b).

Those who argued for the closure of the meat-salting factories tended to imagine cities such as London and Paris as urban centres that had successfully managed industrial pollution and were therefore a step forward compared to Buenos Aires in their fight against epidemic disease. Anti-*saladero* advocates used these references as examples for Buenos Aires to follow. They framed the pollution caused by meat factories as a national embarrassment that degraded the Argentine capital and its inhabitants, placing them at the bottom of an imagined global hierarchy of cities in which the major European imperial capitals occupied the top positions. Following this argument, the *saladeros* condemned the city to a position of subordination, especially with regard to Western European cities. The positive urban vision propagated by opponents of the *saladeros* was that of a city that they imagined as already partially existing in Europe, a healthy environment adorned with abundant green spaces and safe from the threats embodied by industry. Environmental deterioration resulting in epidemics and the growth of an unruly, possibly infectious working-class population were among the main elements of the horror scenario they regarded as connected to industry.

Commentators who argued in favour of the continued operation of the meat-salting factories in the city interpreted both the factories and the role of industry in a rather different fashion. They viewed the path to wealth as passing through industry and, although the factories of Buenos Aires differed from those in London and Paris at the time, they were part of a necessary path of development that the city had to follow. If, in the arguments of the anti-*saladero* faction, the meat-salting factories were places of contamination, violence, and moral decay, they instead enjoyed a completely contrasting role in the eyes of the pro-*saladero* discussants. For instance, they regarded the image of the smoking chimneys as symbols of prosperity as opposed to a representation of decay. They also felt that the inhabitants of Buenos Aires could become prosperous only through the development of industry, which implied morality and health as its direct consequences. Pollution was therefore the expected result of the positive process of urbanisation through industrialisation and the sign that Buenos Aires had chosen the correct path. Imagining Buenos Aires as playing catch-up to its European and American counterparts, one of the key advocates for the *saladeros*, the chemist Miguel Puiggari, affirmed, 'what has happened in all of the major cities such as Paris, London, Berlin, Vienna, Brussels, and New York ... is happening now to us'. According to Puiggari, industrial pollution, population growth, faster means of transportation, and epidemics were all disturbing but nonetheless necessary ingredients of the urban modernity that cities in Europe and North America had already achieved and whose problems they had, for the most part, been able to solve (Puiggari 1871, 45–6).

One of the key discursive devices used both by supporters and detractors involved assessing either the progressiveness or the backwardness of the *saladeros* by placing them in relation to positive Western European and North American models and negative Mediterranean and African models. Buenos Aires' meat-salting factories may have shared few features with British, French, or Central European steel-and-coal or textile industries, yet *saladero* supporters considered them a local declination of the same kind of industrialisation process that had taken place in Europe. *Saladero* opponents instead developed an imaginary of European cities as pleasant, unpolluted, and healthy urbanity. The form in which both parties in the *saladero* controversy referred to European cities served to construct an image of Paris and London, for instance, as cities that had solved the issues of pollution caused by industrialisation. *Porteño* elites were not interested in looking into the fact that discussions on industrial pollution and their correlation with the outbreak of epidemic disease were simultaneously taking place in Western and Central Europe, in some cases even more controversially than in Buenos Aires.

Notwithstanding their contrasting positions in the matter of industrial pollution, *porteño* elites used references to imaginaries of European cities to legitimise their positions. The way cities such as London and Paris had tackled epidemic crises, most notably cholera, were enormously influential in defining the approach with which Buenos Aires was supposed to face an outbreak of epidemic disease. However, this influence did not really have a precise shared meaning and contrasting parties mobilised the same urban models, presented in contrasting ways, to argue for opposed solutions to the epidemic crises. Therefore, on one hand, the cities that had already faced the challenge of cholera theoretically had a major influence on the cities that followed. However, the interchangeability with which the examples of London and Paris could be mobilised for opposing arguments points to the fact that rationales for tackling epidemic crises were also deeply entrenched in local economic interests, fears, and aesthetic conceptions. The example of cholera in Buenos Aires and the discussion it triggered on the meat-salting industry reveals much about the specific position of Buenos Aires' elites and their ways of referring to European cities as models; despite not pertaining to specific content, *porteño* elites bestowed powerful positions of prominence on cities such as Paris and London. These cities were thought of as being ahead on the path Buenos Aires had to follow. Furthermore, abstracting from the specific context of Buenos Aires, the *porteño* reaction to the cholera and yellow fever epidemics illustrates the ambiguous nature of the influence that cities facing comparable challenges in similar times could have on each other. The examples of Paris and London, which had shown themselves to be completely unable to solve dramatic problems such as industrial pollution and cholera in the 1860s, were directly transferred and applied in other contexts but were decisively reinterpreted and constructed in different local contexts.

3 Plague

In the imaginary of a sizeable proportion of those living on the European continent, the plague remains symbolic of epidemic disease par excellence and represents a central reference point for each of the following epidemics that have affected the region since the mid-fourteenth century. Although the last major outbreaks of the plague were registered in Europe in the eighteenth century, the imaginary related to the disease is still enormously powerful (Brook 2020). For instance, at the beginning of the COVID-19 pandemic, the vocabulary and sanitary measures adopted by several governments resembled many of the regulations put in place in long foregone plague epidemics. The word *quarantine*, later replaced by the expression 'lockdown', the creation of 'red zones', restrictions on the movement of people and goods, and the fumigation of streets, as well as concerns regarding food supplies all followed the traditional responses to the plague. In virtually each outbreak of new diseases, such as the emergence of AIDS in the 1980s or cholera in the nineteenth century, the first reflex of governments and populations has often been to resort to the reassurance provided by drastic anti-plague measures. Methods tuned to respond to the plague, the quintessential epidemic catastrophe, have been reproduced in following epidemics for centuries and are conveyed in the present as a first resort in tackling emerging epidemic diseases.

This phenomenon is certainly linked to the influence of the plague in Eurasia, a statement that is hard to overestimate. From the mid-fourteenth century until the eighteenth century, the plague not only spurred the creation of specific sanitary measures, but affected virtually every aspect of life. Even though it would certainly be inaccurate to consider the disease as the sole explanation for macro-historical processes, its impact on demographic, cultural, political, and material history, especially of late medieval and early modern Europe, was vast. Throughout the four centuries of the so-called second pandemic, almost every generation in Europe experienced at least one plague outbreak. During the so-called Black Death, when the plague spread across late medieval Europe between 1346 and 1353, more than one third of the European population succumbed to the disease. The productive and political systems of many regions on the continent were devastated and radically reorganised following the Black Death (Cantor 2001; McNeill 1998; Scheidel 2018). It is probably due to this huge influence, stretched across four centuries and portrayed in a series of literary and historiographic accounts, that the plague still holds its powerful aura and is frequently employed as a metaphor for general political and social collapse (Eisenberg and Mordechai 2020).

The dramatic course taken by the disease, in terms of both the number of infected victims and their environment, has certainly led to the bubonic plague's role as a recurring historical and literary trope. For instance, in cities, the sudden mass dying of rats, which precedes the passage of the plague to humans, as Albert Camus described in his 1947 novel, *The Plague*, is part of its shockingly catastrophic imaginary – a universal disaster that affects not only humans, but also their environment. Indeed, the plague has an overly complex multispecies aetiology that became clearer only at the turn of the twentieth century. The infection through the bacterium *Yersinia pestis* is in fact the last step in a cycle involving a number of species, most notably several types of rodents and fleas. The complex ecological connection between humans, fleas, rats, and *Yerstina pestis* was described by Paul-Louis Simond in 1898 and ignored by the scientific community after its first publication for at least a decade.

Contemporary epidemiology considers the plague as primarily an enzootic, thus a disease that is endemic to a non-human population. In the third pandemic, which has endured from the nineteenth century until today, the disease has spread among several species of wild rodents across the globe that represent the disease's permanent reservoir. Under certain circumstances, the enzootic can become a zoonosis, namely a disease that crosses species barriers, eventually infecting humans. The 'jump' between species usually occurs if humans come into close contact with infected rodents, either because they directly enter wild rodents' habitats, while hunting, for instance, or because wild rodents come closer to human settlements under specific factors of environmental pressure and make contact with 'domestic' rodents, which in turn make close contact with humans. 'Domestic' rodents such as rats, however, are usually unable to directly pass the disease to humans, which is mostly carried by a vector, most likely fleas. Several flea species, including lice and human fleas, can transmit the disease, but only *Xenopsylla cheopis* can transmit it efficiently and is usually responsible for the 'jump' from rodents to humans. When this specific type of rat flea becomes infected by biting an infested rodent, the bacteria block the functioning of its digestive system. With its intestines blocked, the flea cannot assimilate the ingested blood and, in an effort not to starve, it jumps desperately from host to host. While biting several victims, mostly rodents and occasionally other mammals including humans, the sick parasite regurgitates the bacteria clumped in its intestines and infects the host. Furthermore, the plague often kills rats, enhancing the starving flea's need to find other warm animal hosts. Direct human-to-human contagion is mostly connected to airborne infection droplets caused by a specific form of plague, the pneumonic plague. Though it may be less the case today, human-to-human contagion may have played a relevant epidemiologic role in previous plague epidemics, especially during the so-called Black Death and in the following outbreaks of the second plague pandemic (Whittles and Didelot 2016).

Before the large-scale development of antibiotic therapies in the second half of the twentieth century, the disease was utterly cruel and remarkably deadly to human beings. The plague manifests in three main forms: the pneumonic, the septicaemic, and the bubonic. The highly contagious pneumonic form is almost always fatal without antibiotic treatment and clinically resembles any other kind of severe lung infection. The two further forms are transmitted by flea bites. The septicaemic is the rarest of the three forms, which causes an infection of the blood and thus the blackening of the extremities, such as the fingers or nose, and haemorrhages. Without antibiotic treatment, this form is also nearly always lethal. The most frequent form, the bubonic, presents the typical buboes, swollen and blackened lymph nodes, usually in the groin, armpits, neck, or generally in areas close to the infecting flea bite. It causes high fever, intense thirst, cramps, and seizures and is fatal to slightly more than half of those infected if untreated. Before the discovery of the complex multispecies aetiology of the disease, this varied range of manifestations and forms contributed to a high degree of confusion among observers, heightening doubts on the contagiousness of the disease. Likewise, the seemingly arbitrary temporal delay between the outbreak of singular cases, determined by the fact that fleas can fast for several weeks before biting and thus infecting other victims, added further disorientation. Moreover, the disease expanded geographically rather irregularly, following the routes of rats travelling independently, in ships, or generally in all maritime and terrestrial means of transportation concerning the shipment of cereals, one of their favourite sources of nutrition. The migration of rats for environmental reasons, humans travelling along commercial routes, and the movement of armies which carried food supplies along with rats and fleas, were typical opportunities for the disease to spread over large distances.

In addition to the puzzlement engendered by the complex epidemiologic and clinic patterns in contemporary observers of the disease, historians face a further possible source of confusion in an analysis of the plague. In fact, highlighting its exceptional symbolic relevance once more, the word 'plague' has been often used as a generic term to designate every epidemic disease, especially those with high morbidity and lethality. This confusion especially concerns the outbreaks that preceded the identification of the causing agent of bubonic plague at the end of the nineteenth century. For instance, the Plague of Athens in the fifth century BCE, which played a big influence on the Hippocratic corpus and therefore on the later understanding of the plague, was highly unlikely to be caused by what we presently call the plague. Due to examination of DNA in the dental pulp of victims found during archaeological excavations in a mass grave connected to the Plague of Athens, it has only recently been possible to identify typhoid fever as the probable disease that caused the dramatic outbreak of death in ancient Athens (Papagrigorakis et al. 2006).

The developments in DNA examinations in recent decades has helped to clarify confusion concerning the history of the plague in general and to determine with greater certainty that the disease has affected humanity in three big pandemic waves in the past two millennia. The first documented major epidemic that initiated the first pandemic was the Plague of Justinian, named after the eastern Roman emperor who ruled during the period of the disease's expansion in the Mediterranean Basin. Its first clearly documented outbreak occurred in 541 CE in the Egyptian port of Pelusium on the north-eastern edge of the Nile Delta. Even though the original location of the disease is not clear, it ravaged parts of Africa, Asia, and Europe in succeeding waves in the following two centuries, leaving behind an unquantifiable number of victims. Several modern authors see one of the main motors responsible for the end of antiquity in this first pandemic and the large migration flows that accompanied it. For instance, the decimation of the indigenous populations assisted the settlement of the Langobards in Italy, different Slav groups in the Balkans, and Arab expansion in the Middle East (Little 2007). However, in the tricky business of determining macro-historical causation, it is hard to certifiably assert that the last great migrations marking the end of antiquity can be counted among the effects of the plague. Alternatively, it could be argued that the shifts in the distribution, communication, and transportation patterns of human populations in Eurasia and Africa had begun long before the sixth century CE and represented the causal factors that facilitated the expansion of the plague across Afro-Eurasia in the first place.

Major changes in the patterns of human movements and communication seem to have also been related to the emergence of the second bubonic plague pandemic, the most widely known and studied expansion of the disease. As the aetiology of the disease is rather complex, including numerous species of rodents and fleas, the hypotheses on how the plague spread across Eurasia and Africa are also numerous and intricate. Even though a precise determination of a causality chain cannot be clearly established, central factors can be identified that coincide with the emergence and recurrence of plague epidemics between the fourteenth and eighteenth centuries. For instance, the increase in communication and transportation between the densely populated Mediterranean Basin and China, facilitated by the Mongol empire in the thirteenth century, played a decisive role in the development of the pandemic (Green 2020b). At its moment of greatest expansion stretched over an enormous region reaching from China to Eastern Europe and the Mediterranean, the Mongol empire established rapid terrestrial methods of transport that crossed the steppes of Central Asia, which were inhabited by a number of species of wild rodents that may have been established as animal reservoirs of the disease. Other factors such as political turmoil in China at the end of Mongol hegemony in the fourteenth century, rapid urbanisation on the European continent, a series of climatic changes that caused famine in Europe and the movement of reservoir rodent populations escaping from flood and drought in Central Asia, the enhancement of maritime connection between the Mediterranean and Atlantic Ocean all contributed to enabling the plague to spread across Afro-Eurasia. Several populations in this vast geographic area recorded notably high death tolls. In the European case, the continent needed approximately a century and a half to return to the demographic levels that preceded the outbreak of the Black Death in the mid-fourteenth century. In a similar vein to the first plague pandemic, which arguably prompted the end of the ancient world, the second plague pandemic has been viewed as one of the main elements that brought the European Middle Ages to an end (Echenberg 2007; Herlihy 1997; McNeill 1998). With the end of the Middle Ages, however, the disease did not disappear from the European continent and the high mortality rates it engendered failed to subside substantially. In fact, some of the most devastating episodes of the disease took place in the seventeenth and eighteenth centuries, such as the Italian Plague of 1629–30 and the Great Plague of 1665–6 in London, as well as the epidemic in Marseille between 1720 and 1722 (Biraben 1975; Calvi 1989; Cipolla 1981; Moote and Moote 2004). The plague of 1743 in Messina is usually regarded as the last major plague outbreak in the context of the second pandemic in Europe.

Indeed, during the mid-eighteenth century, the plague probably retreated largely to its rodent hosts for at least several decades. By the mid-nineteenth century, the disease began a new wave of global expansion, the so-called third plague pandemic. In contrast to the previous two pandemics, the third was not limited to Afro-Eurasia. The first geographic focus of the third pandemic was the south-western Chinese province of Yunnan, where the disease most likely began to spread from the late eighteenth century onwards. From Yunnan, the disease travelled slowly towards the east in the mid-nineteenth century, following the routes of troops and merchants and eventually reaching the Pearl River Delta and its major urban centres of Canton and Hong Kong in 1894 (Benedict 1996). From the richly trafficked colonial port of Hong Kong, the disease set sail and spread quickly in all directions, following the routes of maritime connections. Unlike previous pandemics, rats could board larger and faster steamboats than ever before at the turn of the twentieth century, a novelty which dramatically accelerated the global spread and geographic reach of the plague.

The disease was first recorded in 1898 in Bombay and other parts of South Asia, which became the region with the highest number of cases, causing the death of approximately twelve million people over the first two decades of the twentieth century. The disease also appeared in many maritime and fluvial port cities around the turn of the century, such as Porto, Buenos Aires, Rio de Janeiro, San Francisco, Glasgow, and Naples, triggering epidemics that did not have the magnitude of the Asian cases (Echenberg 2007; Snowden 2019). Since this wave of expansion at the turn of the twentieth century, the plague has conquered every continent and become endemic among wild rodent populations, especially in geographic areas with a prevalence of wide prairies, such as the United States, Argentina, Brazil, and Central Asia. The pandemic remains ongoing, even though its presence substantially waned from the mid-twentieth century onwards. In the past decade, the most consistently affected region has been Madagascar, where the disease has appeared seasonally in its most contagious pneumonic form.

3.1 Hong Kong: Plague and the Conflict over Circulation

When plague broke out in Hong Kong in 1894, the port city had been a British colony for more than five decades. Located at the south-eastern edge of the densely populated region of the Pearl River Delta, the island had been ceded to the British empire in 1842 following its military victory over the Qing empire in the First Opium War. Under British rule, the city rapidly developed into the main colonial entrepôt of the region, serving as a global hub for a series of wide-ranging commercial exchanges. In 1860, French and British success in the Second Opium War ensured further possibilities for the British colony in terms of territorial and commercial expansion; between 1887 and 1896, almost half of Chinese exports passed through Hong Kong. Resulting from its commercial and financial position, the former fishing village had a population of circa 220,000 inhabitants in 1891, according to the somewhat underestimated figure in the official census. The majority of the city's inhabitants were Chinese, mostly employed as labourers. Following the crisis caused by the Taiping Rebellion in the 1850s, however, a consistent group of wealthy Chinese merchants left mainland China to establish themselves in Hong Kong. In 1894, non-Chinese Hong Kongers made up roughly 12,000 of the population, comprising the ruling group of British government officials and affluent merchants, as well as newly admitted British subjects such as Parsees and Jews from India and the Middle East. Other ethnic groups were also included in the non-Chinese minority such as Sikhs, who were recruited in British India to join the Hong Kong police corps, and other small communities of mainly American, Portuguese, German, and Japanese merchants (Echenberg 2007, 19–20).

Though the city could certainly boast of luxurious residences in the higher-end districts where the small ruling minority dwelled when the plague took root on the island, the greatest part of the urban population lived in rather precarious conditions. In fact, whereas the sanitation movement had consistently contributed to the reshaping of cities in the British Isles from the mid-nineteenth century onwards, Hong Kong had undergone no urban reform – for instance, the city had no sanitation board until the early 1880s. Even then, reform attempts were dwarfed by the conflated interests of European merchants and Chinese landlords, who feared the loss of cheap labour and convenient rent revenues (Chu 2013). Labour regulations and housing policies were virtually non-existent and a sizeable part of the population worked under conditions of exploitation, as a result living in the open air or sharing overcrowded housing, most notably in the lower district of Taipingshan. To protect military and colonial elites from the threat posed by allegedly uncivilised Chinese living habits, colonial rulers resorted to a formal system of ethnic segregation. In 1889, the colonial government passed the European District Reservation Ordinance, aimed at preventing Chinese residents from settling in the upper districts of the city, reserving them and their superior ventilation for the island's European communities. As with other cities under colonial rule, this segregationist policy inspired a certain disinterest in the ruling elites for the health of the local working classes (Arnold 1993, 96–8). Mostly based on miasmatic theories, they surmised that ventilation and a safe distance from possible epidemic foci would keep colonial and commercial elites unscathed from the threat of disease.

In the case of the plague, the assumption of the colonial government proved largely accurate. Of the official yet highly underestimated 2,500 deaths caused by the disease in 1894, only 11 were classified as of European descent. The overwhelming majority of victims were ethnic Chinese, who were especially concentrated in the densely inhabited lower neighbourhoods of Kennedy Town and Taipingshan. However, the colonial government had failed to account for the fact that the news of a port city affected by a widely feared disease such as bubonic plague jeopardised the port's reputation. If the colonial imagination ascribed cholera to the domain of the barbaric, the plague was regarded as a disease belonging to a pre-modern past, which risked bringing into question the modernity of Hong Kong and of the whole British empire alike. Furthermore, ship captains began to take the pragmatic step of avoiding Hong Kong, causing huge economic losses.

Plague therefore forced the British authorities to act, despite contravening their customary non-interventionist policy in the domain of public health in what they perceived to be the internal affairs of the Chinese community. Leaving its traditional laissez-faire policy behind, the colonial government put a series of anti-plague measures in place that prompted major conflicts with the city's Chinese majority. Following the international pronouncement of Hong Kong as an infected port in May 1894, the British authorities adopted a heavy-handed policy to contain the spread of the disease, which mainly revolved around the strict isolation of those infected. Anchored in the city's port, the medical ship *Hygeia* was declared a floating lazaretto that would be employed to isolate plague patients from the rest of the island's population. Troops were sent into poorer Chinese neighbourhoods to carry out house-to-house inspections that aimed to identify the sick and forcibly transfer them onto the floating lazaretto while sanitizing their homes. The Chinese population perceived these operations as an outrageous affront to their medical and religious traditions and to their customary prerogatives (Yip, Liang, and Huang 2016, 16–20).

From a medical perspective, the isolation of the sick was at odds with the principles of the so-called Warm Factor Medical School, the most widely accepted in south-eastern China at the time of the outbreak of plague in Hong Kong. Consistent in their correspondences with miasmatism, Warm Factor theories highlighted the influence of the environment on the body, drawing attention to connections between polluted environments and the spread of disease. For instance, both Warm Factor physicians and miasmatists described the plague as a disease that rose from the soil. Proof of this supposition was provided by the observation that the disease first struck rats due to the fact that their habitat was in closer contact with the earth than that of humans. According to Warm Factor explanations, infected rats escaping from the empoisoned soil frantically looked for water, eventually intruding in cisterns and contaminating the water supply destined for human consumption. Chinese anti-plague responses based on this theory mainly consisted of cleaning homes and of being on guard against the presence of rats. In a similar vein to the measures adopted by the European sanitation movement, it was also essential to avoid stagnant water, to immediately bury dead rats, and to limit the number of people in one room. Warm Factor physicians also advised people to leave cities and find respite in the countryside, a recommendation that was heeded by a great number of Hong Kongers as soon as news spread of the outbreak. Chinese Warm Factor physicians could agree with many of the measures endorsed by contemporary miasmatist Western physicians, and, as with their Western counterparts, considered the isolation of the sick a largely useless strategy (Benedict 1996, 107–9).

As in Europe, isolation was considered a disruption to moral and religious order, which stated that the sick should remain with their families. What is more, confinement on the lazaretto ship brought into question the authority of the Chinese merchant elites of Hong Kong, who had established a philanthropic institution for the poor, the Donghua Hospital, in 1872. The charitable organisation had become an influential institution in the Chinese community and customarily served as mediator between the colonial administration and the wider Chinese population. As the outbreak of the plague began to worsen, the directorate of the Donghua, offering its patients traditional Chinese therapies and refusing to separate the sick from their families, regarded itself as the designated manager of the community's anti-plague efforts. The model of interpreting the plague among British administrators had, however, changed markedly in the years immediately preceding the outbreak of the epidemic in 1894; besides miasmas and 'filth', they also came to view direct human contagion as among the factors that caused the spread of the disease. More precisely, they were convinced that the plague was a contagious 'filth' disease, which they imagined to be directly connected to the living habits of the Chinese community. Therefore, in their eyes, the measures to contain the plague could not be directly entrusted to the Donghua and instead had to explicitly target Chinese residents, their homes, and their belongings. In the most dramatic moments of the epidemic, the British administration ordered the establishment of a militarily enforced sanitary cordon around the perimeter of the Chinese neighbourhood of Taipingshan in order to prevent people from leaving the colony and to ensure strict segregation between Europeans and Chinese.

Led by the directorate of the Donghua, Chinese Hong Kongers organised fierce opposition to both the anti-plague measures and the sanitary cordon. When the situation appeared to be almost out of hand for the greatly outnumbered British officials, the British decided to back off and seek a compromise. The government decided that the sick were not to be brought onto the lazaretto ship but instead to a Chinese-style hospital under the control of the Donghua. Moreover, people were again allowed to leave the colony and the Donghua was permitted to organise ships to bring the sick to Canton, from where they could reach their places of origin. In the immediate aftermath of the end of the epidemic of 1894, after the conflict had passed its highest moment of tension, British administrators ordered the complete demolition of Taipingshan, pushing a part of the poorest population of the city to construct even more precarious shacks on the outskirts of the city, even farther from the European neighbourhoods.

In the case of Hong Kong, where the disease returned on an almost annual basis from 1894 until 1929, the British elites persisted in their racial prejudice towards the Chinese, who were deemed culpable for the plague, without tackling overcrowding and unsanitary living conditions. The colonial authorities, who had always embraced a laissez-faire policy and were not overly interested in the urban space of Hong Kong, wanted to prevent the plague from damaging the functioning of the city as a commercial entrepôt. The attempts of British governors mainly revolved around distinguishing between the flow of ships, capital, and goods on one hand, all of which were vital to their commercial interests, and the movement of Chinese subjects on the other, who allegedly carried the plague and therefore endangered the smooth continuation of commercial flows. This attempt to distinguish between wanted and unwanted circulation failed as the British minority lost the support of the Chinese elites who were not willing to support the anti-Chinese course of the colonial government. The governors quickly realised that there was no way to keep control of the city and backed down in an effort to avoid further confrontation (Benedict 1996, 137–49; Peckham 2016, 82–9).

3.2 Bombay: The Plague in the Imperial Showcase City

Unlike Honk Kong, a recently built city, when plague broke out in Bombay (today Mumbai) in 1898, the port city had been an important urban centre for many centuries. One of the city's seven islands, forming an archipelago off the western coast of the Indian subcontinent, had developed into a relevant trade station from the fourteenth century onwards. In the sixteenth century, the Portuguese acquired the area, gave it the name Bom Bahia – Good Bay – from which the English name Bombay derives, and established a trading post on the archipelago. During the seventeenth century, control over the islands and their conveniently deep natural harbour passed to the English crown and soon after to the East India Company, which established one of its main headquarters there. During the eighteenth century, the diverse population of the trading post began to grow consistently and, by the end of the century, large-scale projects had been initiated in order to reclaim the land between the seven islands, a process which transformed the archipelago into a single landmass by the end of the nineteenth century. The growth of both the city's population and surface area ran parallel to the East India Company's territorial expansion on the

Indian subcontinent, which in turn enhanced connections between Bombay and its surrounding regions.

From the mid-nineteenth century connections between Bombay and the rest of India were boosted by the rapid expansion of the Indian railway network, the first segment of which was inaugurated in Bombay in 1853. Through the development of the railway, the city gained quick and direct access to the surrounding regions that provided Bombay's industries with both cheap labour and raw materials, most notably cotton. When the export of cotton from the southern United States was blocked in the 1860s as a consequence of the American Civil War, Bombay's colonial cotton entrepreneurs seized the chance to transform the city into one of the main global producers and markets for cotton and cloth. The rise of Bombay as an industrial centre was also accompanied by an improvement in its symbolic position within the British empire, attracting a consistent flow of public and private capital. If Hong Kong was a trading post where the British state and British capital made virtually no direct investments in urban infrastructure, Bombay had become home to several major public buildings and institutions by the end of the nineteenth century, such as the gigantic neo-Gothic main station, Victoria Terminus. Fusing the size and style of an English Gothic cathedral with elements of modern railway engineering, the impressive size and architecture of the train station demonstrated the modernity and wealth of Bombay, along with other colonial buildings constructed in the last quarter of the nineteenth century.

That Bombay of all cities was struck by the plague soon became a thorn in the side of the British administration. If the outbreak of the plague could be blamed on the Chinese population in Hong Kong, and on the vicinity of Canton and other Chinese settlements, the situation was markedly different in Bombay. The city was considered one of the most emblematic modern urban showcases of the British empire. More associated with the Middle Ages and early modernity, the plague was generally regarded as a shameful disease that had no place in modernity. The fact that this disease 'of the past' appeared in Bombay, where the British empire was particularly keen to exhibit its modernity, was therefore seen as a blow against the civilising aspirations of the empire. Furthermore, the railway, imagined as the symbol of the British civilising mission in India and the motor behind the colonial modernisation of the country, became one of the main vectors in the spread of the disease to vast swathes of the Indian subcontinent. The role of the modern railway in spreading such a 'backward' disease further challenged the colonial administration, which did not rule out intervention by brutal means in the hope of controlling the disease in Bombay and its surrounding regions (Peckham 2016, 127–38).

Away from the gleam of the public buildings of the colonial administration, the plague found fertile ground in Bombay, as shown by the regular outbreaks of the disease from 1896 until the 1920s, with yearly casualties in the tens of thousands. One of the reasons behind the first outbreak and its continued recrudescence was the overwhelming poverty and precarious living conditions of most of the city's population. Most of the working population, including the workers employed in the mills who alone accounted for one tenth of the overall urban population of 800,000, could only afford housing in the so-called *chawls*, tenement houses where a great number of people lived in small spaces with neither ventilation nor access to water and sewage facilities. In the neighbourhoods in which most tenement houses were located, the number of people per acre amounted to more than three times that of the most crowded working-class neighbourhoods in London (Echenberg 2007, 48).

The plague began to take root in Bombay in 1896, most probably carried by rats travelling onboard a ship from Hong Kong. In the most classic of plague scripts, the first to be affected were rats, which died in great numbers, especially in the area surrounding the port. In the first months of the epidemic, the authorities attempted to deny that the plague had begun to take hold in Bombay. In September 1896, the first case was eventually officially diagnosed in the Mandvi district, where both *chawls* and grain warehouses were located, a favourite haven for rats. Soon after the news that plague was present in Bombay, a significant percentage of the population fled the city. By February 1897, approximately 400,000 people, half of the original population, had left. Many travelled by train to their villages of origin, contributing to the further spread of the disease into the countryside and other cities. This huge exodus was not only the result of the fear generated by the disease, but was most likely due to the threat posed by colonial authorities' enforcement of drastic anti-plague measures.

Although the bacteria responsible for the disease had been identified during the plague epidemic in Hong Kong, the reasons for its spread were still unclear in 1896. The authorities resorted to traditional draconian anti-plague policies from the early modern tradition of the second pandemic. Formalised in the Epidemic Diseases Act of 1897, the list of measures included quarantine, the isolation of the infected in lazarettos, the deportation of their families into isolation camps, quick burial of the dead, and the organisation of home calls, as well as burning the belongings and sometimes the homes of the sick. Members of the newly formed vigilance committee had the right to enter any building and remove the sick, who were forcibly taken to the dreaded Arthur Road pest house. The committee organised search groups to enter homes unannounced and strip search residents, looking for signs of the disease.

When these groups found a case of plague, the whole house was marked with a sign, the sick were brought to a pest house, and all of those living in the same residence as the sick were deported to a 'health camp'. The sign outside the house meant that the sanitary authorities had to visit the house again and decide on the next course of action. This could range from burning the belongings of the sick, to the destruction of walls or the roof to allow air and light to penetrate the building, to the burning of the entire housing facility. Considering the new findings on the rodent-flea nexus, which were acknowledged years after the first outbreak, the practice of burning houses actually enhanced the spread of the plague; terrified by the flames, entire colonies of rodents fled burning houses, taking plague-carrying fleas with them (Snowden 2019, 344–8).

Such anti-plague measures not only prompted the flight of a sizeable number of residents, causing the city's population to decrease notably towards the end of the 1890s, but they also inspired massive resistance and, in some cases, full-blown riots. The biggest of these confrontations occurred in the working-class neighbourhood of Madanpura in March 1898. Following an attempt to hospitalise the daughter of a Muslim weaver, a crowd of several hundred gathered to protest the anti-plague measures. The situation escalated and eventually the British troops opened fire on the crowd, killing twelve protesters. As a result, an even larger group of protesters marched to the lazaretto on Arthur Road. A symbol of the removal of the sick from their homes, the plague hospital was eventually burned down by the marchers, a diverse group consisting of Parsees, Hindus, and Muslims alike who put aside their traditional religious divisions. Though Muslim and Hindu workers had attacked each other during protests only a few years earlier, in 1893, the conditions caused by the plague had succeeded in enabling a new coalition that reunited workers in protesting against both anti-plague measures and working conditions in the mills: anti-plague riots often spilled over into strikes in the textile mills and vice versa. In Bombay, the plague in fact prompted a great shift in the relationship between millowners and millworkers. Due to the exodus of huge numbers of the city's residents as a result of the epidemic, the mills were faced with a scarcity of labour and their owners were forced to offer improved working conditions to their employees. As the epidemic did not begin to abate until the second decade of the twentieth century, the supply of labour continued to be an issue for employers. Conversely, workers steadfastly refused to renounce the hard-earned improvements to their working conditions acquired during the dramatic first year of the epidemic. Furthermore, the riots of the last years of the nineteenth century had shown that in fighting millowners and the colonial administration, an alliance of workers above and beyond traditional religious divisions was not only possible, but also highly successful (Sarkar 2014).

Apart from its long-term effects in prompting the creation of working-class anti-colonial sentiment, in the short term, the riots of March 1898 also pushed the colonial administration in Bombay to change its strategy in fighting the plague. Soon after the riot of March, which was replicated a short time afterwards in other cities and villages in the region, the colonial administration began to fear that it had to tackle not only the spread of the plague, but also growing revolt against their rule. On one hand, a system of political repression was enforced; several newspapers were closed down and alleged agitators were deported, for instance. On the other hand, the compulsory measures regarding the removal of the sick from their homes were abolished in large cities, including Bombay, where the small contingent of British troops could not be sure of maintaining order in case of an uprising. Furthermore, from a medical point of view, the Indian Plague Commission entrusted with studying the epidemic released a trailblazing report that concluded that the brutal measures adopted in the previous years had largely been useless, and may have in fact worsened the epidemic. Nonetheless, the plague commission initially refuted Paul-Louis Simond's 1898 explanation that the plague spread via the rat-flea nexus. Therefore, forcible eviction and isolation were abandoned and the colonial authorities concentrated on applying sanitation principles, aiming to create wide boulevards between the city's densely inhabited working-class neighbourhoods. Only a decade after Simond's paper, the rat-flea nexus was recognised as pivotal in the propagation of the disease and rats became the main target of the new campaign against the plague, the spread of which started declining in the last years of the 1910s.

4 Tuberculosis

Cholera and plague, the diseases analysed in the previous sections, present many differences but nonetheless triggered comparable reactions. Panic and the connected desire to enhance control over the population, for instance, were typical features that accompanied outbreaks of both cholera and the plague, though they took root in different epochs and geographic settings. In fact, the two diseases have substantially contributed to shaping the image of epidemics as moments of deep and intense crisis in which the social order as a whole is questioned and at risk of collapse (Rosenberg 1989). Tuberculosis, the disease under analysis in this section, operated somewhat differently. Primarily a pulmonary disease, tuberculosis caused far more deaths than cholera in the nineteenth century without, however, engendering dramatic reactions. The characteristics of tuberculosis challenge the idea of epidemics as temporally condensed dramatic crises. The reasons for the contrasting reactions caused by tuberculosis are found in the specific features of the disease caused by the *Mycobaterium tuberculosis* in human beings and its diffusion across the globe, as well as the history of the social and cultural understandings of this illness.

The chronology of tuberculosis is based on its development in individuals and populations, which completely differs from the development of cholera and the plague. Patients affected by cholera and the plague usually develop symptoms within days, occasionally within hours, while the symptoms of tuberculosis can develop in an undefined time frame after infection, lasting from a few weeks to decades. In most cases, the immune system responds effectively to the mycobacteria, the infection never awakens from its latency, and patients never develop active tuberculosis, despite having had contact with the bacillus. In other cases, the weakening of the immune system caused by health factors such as bad nutrition, ageing, or other diseases such as AIDS can activate the disease. Once active, tuberculosis usually attacks the respiratory tract and, without treatment, causes a typically slow yet often fatal deterioration of the lungs and the respiratory functions of the body. Patients who develop active tuberculosis also become contagious and spread the droplets carrying the bacilli around them, mainly through coughing. Furthermore, compared with the aggressive nature of cholera and the plague, the first perceivable symptoms of pulmonary tuberculosis, the most common manifestation of the disease, are hardly noticeable at all. They include a rather inconspicuous sense of fatigue, loss of weight, and a cough. In the later stages of the disease, tuberculosis causes the coughing up of bloody sputum – the emblematic symptom of the disease – persistent fever, extreme fatigue, and insomnia. Without treatment, death typically results in half of active tuberculosis patients after long periods alternating between expansion and remission. In the stages of expansion, the disease is utterly debilitating, forcing the sick to bed for long periods of time. These specific characteristics, notably the delayed appearance of symptoms following infection as well as its typically long progress, have come to characterise the disease as a somewhat 'silent' killer. This 'silent' character is especially apparent when compared to cholera and the plague, which almost invariably elicited notable and at times extremely 'loud' reactions wherever they appeared.

Tuberculosis is an ancient disease and has probably been a permanent companion of humanity since the Neolithic age. It has affected Africa, Eurasia, and the American continent from time immemorial. Evidence of the presence of the *Mycobacterium tuberculosis* has been found in Egyptian mummies, in ancient graves in Europe, and in the pre-Columbian Americas. For the most part of its long relationship with humanity, the disease has largely been rather more endemic than epidemic. In other words, it afflicted humans across the globe on a more consistent basis and did not experience dramatic phases of expansion into new and susceptible populations, simply because it has always been virtually omnipresent. Being such an ancient disease, it has also had several names throughout its history such as phthisis and consumption, and it has been described in several sources across a range of eras. The name phthisis, for instance, and the description of symptoms that clearly recall modern tuberculosis originate from the influential treaties of the ancient Greek physician Hippocrates (McMillen 2015).

One of the most relevant descriptions and interpretations of the disease for the period analysed, the so-called romantic theory of consumption, was delivered by René Laënnec, one of the pioneers in using the stethoscope to auscultate and classify respiratory sounds. A member of the Paris School of Medicine, Laënnec viewed consumption as a discrete disease, thus not only as a general bodily imbalance mostly affecting the lungs but also a disease that can attack other organs and regions of the body. Despite this view, he deemed tuberculosis a non-contagious affliction caused by a predisposition embedded in the natural constitution of the individual. He argued that moral influences and especially negative emotions such as grief or unhappy love, or the overuse of intellectual faculties, could activate the underlying disease. In other words, consumption was a mere question of individual destiny that had almost no connection with social origin or behaviour. In contrast to theories concerning other diseases, the romantic theory of consumption liberated the sick from blame or stigmatisation (Barnes 1995).

In stark contrast to the shame and moral stigma associated with cholera, especially among the poor, in Europe, tuberculosis was widely considered a dignified disease during most of the nineteenth century. This interpretation included consumption among one of the typical features of the romantic genius. In men, tuberculosis was seen to engender an intensification of feelings and intellectual activities. Leading romantic artists were, for instance, among the most famous sufferers of consumption. Throughout most of the nineteenth century, this view of tuberculosis elicited the emergence of a proper taste for 'consumptive beauty'. In an intimate connection to gendered imaginaries, fragile literary figures of consumptive women proliferated in the arts. Mimì in Giacomo Puccini's *La Bohème* and Violetta in Giuseppe Verdi's *La Traviata*, two of the most famous nineteenth-century opera heroines, were both affected by consumption. These figures enhanced the attraction of the disease's aesthetic traits, which became a sign of refinement and distinction. Consumptive beauty was so popular in nineteenth-century Europe that it became a matter of fashion. Especially for women, the transformation caused by the disease, such as the elongation of the limbs or the paleness of the skin, became part of the bodily attributes even healthy women were meant to strive for. For instance, a layer of white rice powder on the face and belladonna eye drops conjured an image of anaemia and the wide-eyed look of tuberculosis victims. Carolyn Day defines this fashion canon as 'consumptive chic' (Day 2017). In her book *Illness As Metaphor*, published in 1978, Susan Sontag argues that even the twentieth-century cult of thinness in women's fashion is a continuation of the romantic tradition of tuberculosis (Sontag 1978).

In the wake of these interpretations of tuberculosis and its typically slow and 'silent' clinical progress, it is not surprising that, throughout most of the nineteenth century, the disease never took on the features of an epidemic. Most physicians regarded the disease as non-contagious and preferred to refer its appearance to the constitutional fate of the individual. The disease also caused a slow and respectable death that did not undermine social expectations concerning the end of life, unlike cholera. Against this backdrop, tuberculosis did not spur authorities to opt for radical interventions and did not affect the course of public life, despite causing astounding rates of invalidity and death that greatly surpassed those of cholera. The transformation of tuberculosis into a shameful illness and feared epidemic disease took place following the slow advent of contagionism and germ theory. Initial studies proving the contagious-ness of tuberculosis were delivered by Jean-Antoine Villemin, who successfully inoculated rabbits with the disease in the late 1860s. By isolating and identifying *Mycobacterium tuberculosis* as the microorganism at the root of the disease, Robert Koch provided the ultimate proof of its contagiousness in 1882. However, this discovery did not lead to an immediate change of course, most probably because Koch's finding had no direct outcomes on the therapy of consumption, which became possible only with the development of antibiotics. The romantic interpretation of the disease survived long after the publication of Koch's studies. For instance, Thomas Mann's literary rendition of the disease in *The Magic Mountain*, published in 1924, shows how the disease was still viewed through a heterogenous mix of romantic and bacteriological ideas (Humphreys 1989).

Apart from the changes in medical theory, epidemiological studies undertaken in big cities further contributed to the transformation of attitudes towards tuberculosis. For instance, surveys on consumption and poverty that were regularly carried out in London from the end of the 1880s showed a strong correlation between low income, poor living conditions, and the development of active tuberculosis. Similar surveys in other countries in Europe and on the American continent produced similar results. Consequently, from the last years of the nineteenth century, tuberculosis was not only a romantic disease any-more; it had instead become more widely connected with questions of class and race. In several countries such as Great Britain, France, the United States, Italy, Russia, and Japan, public associations to prevent and fight tuberculosis were established between the early 1890s and 1900s. Against the backdrop of surging nationalism, these institutions managed to interlock the fight against tuberculosis with general concerns on the biopolitical health of the workforce. Discussions on tuberculosis offered an arena in which imaginaries revolving around the reproduction of the workforce were presented as entrenched in general preoccupations concerning the strength of the national body politic (Barnes 1995).

The foundation of anti-tuberculosis associations marked the beginning of a new historical phase in the relationship with tuberculosis. Between the end of the nineteenth century and the mid-twentieth century, when antibiotic therapies emerged, major campaigns were put in place aimed at fighting the disease through prevention. These campaigns played a pivotal role in shaping new ways to organise daily practices and particularly attitudes towards public and private spaces in cities. In the realm of private practices, the campaigns especially targeted women, imagined as defenders of household hygiene from the threat of germs. The 'war on tuberculosis' had a great influence on propagating a normative image of women as middle-class housewives tasked with keeping the danger of tuberculosis, and generally of germs, at bay on a daily basis (Tomes 1999). In the planning of urban public spaces, the 'war on tuberculosis' continued the tradition first formed by the sanitarians while also setting new emphases. Evidence of the airborne character of the disease provided a new bacteriological foundation for the sanitation movement's insistence on circulation as a key element in constructing healthy urban environments. If the construction of underground sewers, a central tenet of the sanitary city, had been the primary concern of nineteenth-century sanitarians, the focus on the steady circulation of air proved more relevant in the fight against tuberculosis. Two typical planning measures aimed at producing a steady airflow in cities were wholeheartedly revived – the creation of large boulevards and the overall effort to reduce population density. Aimed at augmenting the circulation of air while avoiding congestion, these measures proved very convenient from the 1920s onwards, especially in the United States with the rise of the automobile, a new phenomenon that would quickly become a new central protagonist in public urban space.

From the last quarter of the nineteenth century, the emphasis on the benefits of sunlight and air circulation increased and soon became the favourite preventive and therapeutic means to fight tuberculosis. Access to daylight and fresh air were also the grounding principles of the Garden City Movement, one of the most influential turn-of-the-century schools of urban design. Moreover, several main tenets of modernism, both in architecture and urban planning, were directly connected to the idea of allowing a steady flow of air and light to enter not only cities, but also housing facilities. Principles developed in architecture in the 1920s, such as flat roofs, balconies, wide light-catching windows, and access to 'nature', were all elements that served in the last quarter of the nineteenth century as typical features of tuberculosis sanatoria. These were establishments that provided treatment for tuberculosis based on a strict behavioural regime and on exposure to abundant sunlight, fresh air, and to 'nature' in general. Emblematic modernist furniture pieces are direct reinterpretations of typical interior fittings of sanatoria. For instance, the chaise longue was an essential piece of sanatoria equipment that allowed patients to comfortably lay for hours in the open air on sunny balconies and verandas (Campbell 2005).

In continuation with the tradition of the colonial hill stations, the long distances from big cities and the purity of mountain air were usually central factors in determining preferable locations for sanatoria. The idea of 'nature' as a healing force in opposition to the city as a place of disease and contagion was reinforced by a long intellectual tradition, which was consistently revived and boosted by the fight against tuberculosis (Williams 1973). Despite being just one among many factors, concerns around public health and especially tuberculosis were greatly influential in the reinforcement of the anti-urban feelings that accompanied the exodus of the wealthier classes from city centres in countries such as Great Britain, Germany, and the United States while also prompting the rise of mass suburbanisation in North America (Hayden 2003). In its intersection with racial prejudice against African Americans and their allegedly greater susceptibility to catching tuberculosis, anxiety about the spread of the disease also played a pivotal role in cementing and deepening tendencies towards urban racial segregation, most notably in the United States, as the case of Baltimore highlights. Although the following sections discuss two cases on the American continent, the reader may try to keep in mind that tuberculosis has been a virtually ubiquitous disease on all continents to date.

4.1 Baltimore: Tuberculosis, Race, and Segregation

Analysed in depth in Samuel Robert's study *Infectious Fear*, the case of Baltimore provides an excellent illustration of the ways in which medical theories concerning the racial causation of tuberculosis intersected with urban segregation in the United States. In the geographical and political middle ground between abolitionist and slave states, Baltimore developed into one of the most important African American urban centres in the early nineteenth century. Even before the outbreak of the American Civil War in 1861, the city represented a key focal point for free African Americans. Indeed, by the time of the Emancipation Proclamation in 1863, only one tenth of Baltimore's black population was still subject to slavery. In the years following the Civil War, the city continued its legacy as a thriving urban centre with a strong African American component. Although Baltimore's white population of mainly Eastern European immigrants had grown proportionally more than its black counterpart, the city had confirmed its status as one of the African American capitals by the turn of the twentieth century. In 1910, more than 84,000 African Americans resided in the port city on the Chesapeake Bay, a figure that was marginally surpassed nationwide only by nearby Washington, DC (94,000), New York (91,000), and New Orleans (89,000). Moreover, since the mid-nineteenth century, the city had also been an African American centre in terms of culture. Literacy rates among black inhabitants were high throughout the second half of the nineteenth century, for instance. Consequently, Baltimore had a prosperous African American editorial scene and more than thirty daily and weekly newspapers in the second half of the century for the city's black readership (Roberts 2009, 9–10).

Between the mid-nineteenth and mid-twentieth centuries, tuberculosis was a common cause of death in the United States, even more so for urbanites and among non-whites, the vast majority of whom were African Americans. In the 1920s in Baltimore, for instance, tuberculosis mortality reached an average figure of 73.3 yearly deaths per 100,000 among whites, while accounting for 255 yearly deaths per 100,000 non-whites (Roberts 2009, 23–7). Initially, the most widespread hypothesis to explain this state of affairs was centred on the bodily constitution of African Americans, which was allegedly distinct from those of other population groups. Conflated with the tradition of tropical medicine, the rise of 'scientific' racism in the nineteenth century and the related conception of biological races had resulted in the idea of a correlation between contrasting bodily constitutions and race (Harrison 1999). Most notably in the second half of the nineteenth century, American physicians and many of their European counterparts believed that race was a central factor in determining the risk of contracting certain diseases (McMillen 2015), namely tuberculosis in the case of African Americans.

A group of these physicians even imagined the existence of fixed anatomic distinctions between whites and blacks. In the case of tuberculosis, for instance, they asserted that the black population allegedly had smaller 'tropical' lungs than whites, an anatomic difference that exposed them to tuberculosis with more frequency. Even when bacteriology began to propagate more thoroughly in the United States at the turn of the century, white physicians addressing the question mostly clung to racial explanations. One of the most widespread racial arguments of the time stated that the elevated rates of tuberculosis among African

American were no longer tied to their allegedly different bodily constitutions but were rather the result of racial degeneration caused by urban life. They argued that the moral and physical regime of slavery was the most adequate for African Americans and therefore considered the freedom city life granted a cause of the deterioration of the 'black race'. Such arguments remained somewhat popular in the first two decades of the twentieth century, although black scholars pointed out their scientific inconsistency on numerous occasions. African American intellectuals such as the physician M. V. Ball and sociologists W.E.B. Du Bois and Kelly Miller had remarked that, in the light of the emerging evidence concerning the correlation of living conditions and tuberculosis, it was in fact the socio-economic and physical conditions of black Americans, most notably their housing and working situations, which rendered them more susceptible to tuberculosis (Roberts 2009, 46–52).

A more in-depth analysis of the housing situation of African American Baltimoreans clearly shows that their living standards were extremely low in most cases and that segregation played a major role in driving up rates of overcrowding. Until the end of the 1880s, the African American population of Baltimore mostly resided in South Baltimore, an area of the city with limited access to clean water and prey to regular flooding by the polluted waters of the harbour. These unhealthy conditions pushed middle-class black Baltimoreans to look for better housing in the city's north-western districts at the turn of the century. Estate agents used the arrival of African American middle-class families in neighbourhoods with white majorities such as Druid Hill to stir fear among whites that their properties would quickly lose their value due to the presence of the new African American neighbours. The following step in the widespread business model practised by real estate speculators, later known as 'blockbusting', consisted of encouraging white inhabitants acting under the anxiety of property depreciation to sell their homes at a loss and to move to more racially homogenous neighbourhoods. Estate agents could then buy housing at a convenient price and rent it at high rates to African Americans who, in the context of urban racial segregation, had extremely limited chances to choose their place of residence freely (Nightingale 2012, 309). For instance, in the case of South Baltimore, the destruction of a series of residential blocks due to the construction of a train station pushed many black Baltimoreans to look for new homes, which they found in overpriced housing offered by blockbusting developers in the north-western districts. Housing surveys carried out at the beginning of the twentieth century all confirmed that African Americans in Baltimore paid three times as much as whites on average who occupied housing of a similar size and standard (Roberts 2009, 72–5).

Fearing the settling of African Americans in otherwise all-white neighbour-hoods, white property owners formed associations, assuming the racial guard-ianship of neighbourhoods against what they perceived as an invasion of African American Baltimoreans that threatened their housing assets. As a reaction to the growing pressure of these white segregationist associations, Mayor J. Barry Mahool signed an ordinance in 1910 that formally prohibited African Americans from moving onto street blocks with white majorities and vice versa. One of the main arguments backing the municipal ordinance was a study published by the Johns Hopkins Medical School of Baltimore that showed a higher incidence of tuberculosis in housing blocks with African American majorities. Notwithstanding the protests of several physicians, who argued that it was precisely the issue of overcrowding caused by segregation that led to higher rates of tuberculosis among African Americans, the segrega-tionist ordinance was widely promoted as a programme to contain the spread of the disease. Baltimore's segregationist ordinance provided a first example that many cities across the United States emulated in the immediately following years. A successful case was issued by the African American National Association for the Advancement of Colored People against a similar segrega-tionist ordinance in Louisville, Kentucky, that reached the Supreme Court in 1917 and eventually undermined the possibility of perpetuating a system of racial segregation by law. The Supreme Court considered racial zoning as unconstitutional state interference in fundamental property rights and therefore brought an end to formal urban segregation, nonetheless leaving a free hand for the continuation of practices of blockbusting as the great migration of African Americans from the rural states to major industrial cities, including Baltimore, was in full swing. After the ruling of the Supreme Court, Baltimore's new mayor, John Preston, commented that the repeal of the segregationist ordinance was a major backlash in the attempt to maintain the health of the city's white population, most notably a backlash in the fight against tuberculosis (Nightingale 2012, 305–6).

Another key element in the relationship between residential segregation and tuberculosis was the emergence of the so-called house infection theory from the end of the 1880s. Elaborating on the principles of microbiology and largely propagated, this theory reached its peak of success in the first decades of the twentieth century. According to house infection theory, tuberculosis was a contagious disease that could become a fixture in specific environments. Most notably daily practices within private homes were deemed able to link the disease to specific houses and as a result to their inhabitants. The supporters of house infection theory usually advocated for a system of spatial surveillance of the sick, according to which the addresses of patients affected by tuberculosis had to be registered and constantly monitored. Regular inspections of private housing also formed part of the preventive measures proposed by the supporters of house infection theory. Baltimore's City Health Department was among the institutions that embraced this theory and put in place a system of surveillance of consumptive patients towards the end of the nineteenth century. If compulsory reporting of the disease was universal, house calls and inspections only targeted patients living in tenements and boarding houses, as inspectors were usually not allowed to enter the premises of homeowners.

Even though house infection theory essentially refuted the nexus between race and tuberculosis, it became racialised in its implementation and reinforced existing racial segregation. Although house infection theory may not have propagated ideas imagining momentous physical differences among races, it certainly did form the basis for a new kind of stigma tied to cultural racial prejudices. Both house infection theorists and Baltimore's Health Department no longer considered anatomy or the racial deterioration of African Americans to be determinant for tuberculosis, but rather their way of living and daily practices, which were seen as responsible for the spread of the disease. As a result, surveillance measures and house calls in Baltimore, mainly carried out by nurses of anti-tuberculosis associations, clearly targeted African Americans and what white administrators conceived as their unhealthy private household economy, unclean living, and lack of bodily discipline. Even though this house surveillance was the first appearance of a public health policy, its racialised application continued racial stigmatisation and reinforced the already existing segregation that was the main cause of the higher incidence of tuberculosis among African Americans in Baltimore, as many both black and white professionals underlined in this period (Roberts 2009, 85–95). Racial segregation and stigmatisation were responsible for the housing and living conditions that caused higher rates of tuberculosis among African American Baltimoreans in the eyes of many commentators of the first decades of the twentieth century. In a clear example of a vicious circle, it was exactly these higher rates that functioned as one of the main 'objective' arguments that legitimised the very existence and maintenance of clearly defined colour lines in Baltimore in the eyes of the white majority and local government.

4.2 Buenos Aires: Tuberculosis in a Non-segregated City

From the mid-nineteenth century and most notably from the 1880s, Buenos Aires grew from its position as a regional urban centre to become an international commercial hub and the biggest and most populous port city on the western side of the Atlantic Ocean besides New York. While the city's population numbered approximately 200,000 inhabitants at the beginning of the 1870s, there were almost one million *porteños* at the turn of the century. In the twentieth century, Buenos Aires continued its prodigious growth; without including the metropolitan area beyond the confines of the city's federal district, its population had risen to around three million inhabitants by the end of the Second World War. In the hundred years between the mid-nineteenth and mid-twentieth centuries, the reason for such explosive population growth is mainly found in the huge numbers of immigrants, mostly from Europe, but also from other regions of South America. Indeed, one of the characterising features of Buenos Aires' population from the mid-nineteenth century was its sizeable proportion of inhabitants born abroad or in other Argentine provinces, which approached half of the overall population. From the 1880s, not only the propor-tion but the absolute number of immigrants settling in the metropolis on the River Plate grew exponentially. Together with other groups such as Eastern European and Mediterranean Jews, Italians and Spaniards migrated to Buenos Aires in their millions, representing the most important demographic source of the city's prodigious expansion.

When the former Spanish fortress around which the colonial city had devel-oped was completely demolished in the 1880s, followed by the construction of a new port able to accommodate large transatlantic vessels, the city had long begun to expand into the surrounding prairies away from the shores of the River Plate. With the river its most glaring geographic limitation to the east, Buenos Aires expanded to the south, north, and west, substantially enlarging the grid structure of its streets inherited from Spanish colonial tradition. The city's authorities devised initial plans to build major avenues in the 1880s that would slice through parts of the small blocks in the city centre such as the renowned Avenida de Mayo. From the 1870s onwards, the central districts, where many of the tenement houses inhabited by migrants were also located, set out a gradual transformation into a government, commercial, and financial centre, whereas the districts to the north developed into residential areas for the affluent classes. Industrial activities clustered in the south and south-western districts of the city, which were in turn largely inhabited by lower classes. Apart from these areas, in which patterns of functional and class segregation devel-oped as the city grew, the majority of the population lived in less densely inhabited areas or so-called *barrios*, where solid neighbourhood structures emerged. Even though not everybody became a homeowner, middle-class and partially working-class house ownership developed into one of the central motors of Buenos Aires' huge spatial development and constituted the back-bone of these neighbourhoods, which were built increasingly farther from the central districts with the gradual growth of the city's transport network of underground and overground rail services, trams, and omnibuses (Gutiérrez 2013; Moya 1998; Scobie 1992).

As in most cities of comparable size, tuberculosis was among the main causes of death in Buenos Aires until the development of antibiotic therapies in the mid-twentieth century. The development in tuberculosis mortality rates was comparable to that of other major cities; from between 230 and 300 yearly deaths per 100,000 inhabitants during the 1880s, the rate dropped slightly between the 1890s and the 1900s, only to rise once again and remain stable until the beginning of the 1930s. From then on, the mortality rate began to fall regularly and plummeted by the end of the 1940s, when antibiotic therapies became more readily available. At the beginning of the 1950s, the mortality rate for tuberculosis was slightly under 30 per 100,000 inhabitants. Between the 1880s and the 1930s, the aforementioned fluctuations in tuberculosis mortality rates were rather small when compared to the drastic changes in the way the disease was perceived and in its relationship with other prevalent causes of death in the same period. The relevance of other infectious diseases such as cholera and smallpox had declined substantially by the beginning of the twentieth century, while tuberculosis emerged as one of the most common causes of death. By the end of the 1920s, the disease was the second most common cause of death in Buenos Aires (Armus 2011, 10). Changes in the perception of the disease also contributed to this shift in its relevance, especially in the decades following the discovery of its microbiological aetiology in 1882. As in many other cities, knowledge of the infectious nature of the disease made its way to the wider population thanks to a series of noteworthy public campaigns, transforming what had been viewed as an inherited disease triggered by environmental factors into a widely feared contagious disease.

However, despite increasing access to information about the contagious nature of tuberculosis, especially from the turn of the twentieth century onwards, collateral explanations proliferated that were not necessarily alternatives to germ theory, but rather superimposed or intertwined with it. One of the main rationales of these additional theories was that of finding reasons for the uneven distribution of the disease among various groups of the city's inhabitants. Gender, race, ethnicity, and class were among the most common variables used to explain the unequal distribution of the disease. As previously seen in the case of Baltimore, theories focusing largely on racial and ethnical predispositions to tuberculosis were also relatively commonplace in Buenos Aires, at least until the mid-1930s, and mostly conflated with fears concerning the future health of the 'Argentine race'. Though nativists did exist, most Argentine elites conceived the national body as an entity resulting from the merging of different migrant groups. The country's indigenous population, as well as Afro-Argentines and migrants from Africa or Asia, occupied a somewhat marginal role in this discussion as elites embraced the idea of the 'Argentine race' as a mix of different people, provided they were of European descent. Against this backdrop, the debate on the correlation of tuberculosis with specific ethnic and racial groups was often connected with questions linking the idea of regulating the migration of different European populations with a conception of the nation as a body that could be forged following principles of eugenics. That some ethnic groups were more susceptible to contracting tuberculosis was a central element to consider in an assessment of the 'quality' of certain ethnical elements, therefore determining if specific ethnic groups should be accepted or rejected. Practically, controlling the flux of migration was never much more than an unfulfilled fantasy which did nonetheless deliver critical outcomes in creating positive or negative discrimination vis-à-vis specific groups of migrants.

For instance, tuberculosis was a stigma that weighed heavy on the shoulders of Spanish immigrants, especially those arriving from the north-western Spanish region of Galicia. In the early twentieth century, statistics reported that immigrants from Spain were twice as likely to contract tuberculosis as their Italian counterparts. Many experts tackling the problem believed that this was caused by an unknown form of ethnic inheritance and therefore suspected Galician immigrants, who represented the majority of working-class Spaniards in Buenos Aires, not only of possibly spreading the disease to other otherwise healthier groups, but also of causing potential harm to the genetic stock of the 'Argentine race'. Forms of discrimination against Galician immigrants had existed before the emergence of the question of tuberculosis, and the disease was probably not the only reason for the discrimination Galicians faced during this period. Nonetheless, conceptions of the ethnically inherited character of the disease contributed to perpetuating and cementing such prejudice.

If Galicians were the objects of a negative stigma concerning tuberculosis, other ethnic groups such as Basques and Eastern European Jews enjoyed positive discrimination as they were deemed almost immune to tuberculosis. Building on previously existing prejudices, this presumed immunity was connected to the alleged bodily vigour typical of the Basque 'race' in their particular case, which also included some of the most renowned upper-class families of Buenos Aires. In the case of Jewish immigrants, despite being the targets of antisemitic discrimination and being suspected of spreading typhus, they were widely considered almost untouched by tuberculosis at the beginning of the twentieth century. Experts imagined that Jews mostly had a long-standing tradition of life in urban centres, where they had supposedly developed a high resistance to the disease (Armus 2011, 221–50). Notwithstanding the key impact of the imagined correlations between specific ethnic groups, class, and tuberculosis on the type of positive or negative discrimination these groups were subjected to, their impact on the actual constitution of built space is hard to measure. Before tuberculosis rose to occupy a position as a deeply felt public health issue, Buenos Aires was not segregated along ethnic lines, despite evidence of spatial clusters of specific ethnic and regional groups (Baily 2000, 1999; Moya 1998). Tuberculosis did not substantially change this situation and Galicians, for instance, were never relegated to a specific neighbourhood or area of the city.

Class, which certainly intertwined with ethnicity as, for instance, most Galicians were part of the working class and Basques were part of the affluent classes, was nonetheless generally more likely than ethnicity to determine the area of the city in which people lived; concerns regarding the spread of tuberculosis also became visible along the variable of class. Public debate focused on the living conditions of the working classes as a possible cause of tuberculosis, with a particular focus on those living in the tenement houses located in the central districts. Issues concerning these dwellings and their inhabitants had emerged during the previous cholera and yellow fever epidemics of the second half of the nineteenth century (Carbone 2022a). When the danger that these diseases represented seemed to falter at the end of the century, tuberculosis appeared as a new menace lurking in poor houses, placing the spotlight firmly on the tenement houses of the city centre once again.

In the wake of the fight against tuberculosis at the beginning of the twentieth century, the solutions proposed by hygienists bore a very close resemblance to those their colleagues had prescribed in the second half of the nineteenth century. Parks and urban green spaces were deemed central for providing the city with fresh air and sunlight and were furthermore considered as having an educating function that would enable the working classes living in the densely populated city centre to enjoy healthy and morally decent pleasures. As much as the green spaces were regarded as a positive factor, high residential density was considered dangerous. If nineteenth-century hygienists had stressed the problem of high population density when studying private homes, as a certain quantity of air per person was needed to avoid dangerous accumulations of miasma, twentieth-century hygienists tackling tuberculosis stressed slightly different aspects. Sunlight was, for instance, emphasised in a new way, and the perfect hygienic home should have a more direct relationship with the outdoors. Private gardens, balconies, open courtyards, and wide windows that could catch light gained in prominence through a new hygienic conscience based on germ theory. What is more, the idea of building satellite cities in which workers could entertain a more direct relationship with nature enjoyed rising popularity in the first decades of the twentieth century, although they did have a limited impact on Buenos Aires' actual built-up areas. In the specific case of Buenos Aires, the relationship with nature was considered even more significant than elsewhere, as planners thought that both transatlantic and internal migrants originated from rural regions and were thus supposed to need a more direct relationship with their original everyday lives of regular contact with nature (Armus 2011, 322–44). The overall influence of germ theory and tuberculosis on the modern architecture and urban planning movements was significant, and ideals of the modern city mainly revolved around the breaking up of the dense fabric of the nineteenth-century city, allowing fast movement and the penetration of air and sunlight into the city. The outdoors was not planned only in the form of public parks, but also as a space that should be available in private houses, gaining new attention while also fostering previously existing tendencies towards suburbanisation.

Conclusion

Based on the concept that knowledge of disease has been pivotal in shaping the ways in which different societies across a range of epochs have reacted to epidemic challenges, this Element analyses the relationship between medicine, epidemics, and cities in its first part. The knowledge upon which this relationship was built has consistently changed throughout history while maintaining a certain degree of heterogeneity, at least until the first decades of the twentieth century. Indeed, the existence of multiple understandings of disease has perhaps been one of the few constants in the historical relationship between medicine, epidemics, and cities. Since antiquity, theories that saw epidemics as the result of poisoning miasmas have coexisted with notions regarding contagion as the root of disease. In the case of the plague in early modern Europe, a combination of various concepts of disease guided authorities in devising the measures used to control the spread of epidemics. Quarantine, for instance, a concept which maintains a high degree of relevance, was one of the practices based on heterogenous disease theories that was mainly established in cities so as to cope with the plague. Apart from the experience of the plague, European colonialism and the dramatic epidemics it caused also left consistent marks in the way diseases were viewed. Tropical medicine arose as a medical discipline from colonial experiences, which from the nineteenth century increasingly fused emerging racial theories with notions concerning the nature, spread, and possible strategies to contain epidemic disease.

At the beginning of the nineteenth century, the Paris School of Medicine propagated the idea of diseases as discrete entities, prompting a gradual shift away from the hitherto dominant Hippocratic tradition of seeing disease as the result of the imbalance in the ratio of a single patient's bodily fluids. This shift paved the way for the rise of medical statistics and hygiene as a discipline that sought to tackle the social roots of disease, especially in cities. The sanitation movement, which had an enormous influence on the development of cities across the world, built up a set of principles to reform urban space by conflating statistic knowledge, miasmatic theories, and moral notions. In the last quarter of the nineteenth century, the new paradigm of germ theory emerged and gradually became the prevalent theory concerning the causes and spread of disease. The influence of germ theory on cities was initially superimposed onto elements of the sanitation movement, and only from the beginning of the twentieth century did germ theory begin to have a more specific influence on architecture and urban planning, developing into one of the theories at the root of the rise of modernist architecture. With the consolidation of the hegemony of germ theory, heterogeneity in the field of medical aetiology has fallen substantially, though not entirely.

If heterogeneity has been one of the main traits in the history of the relationship between medicine and epidemics, the impact of epidemics on cities was also varied and heterogenous. Indeed, the reconstruction of the history of three major epidemic diseases and their impact on a range of urban centres has shown that the responses these cities gave to global epidemic challenges were different and nonetheless intimately related. As the first and most dreaded of the epidemic diseases to be analysed that emerged in the nineteenth century, cholera caused tremendous waves of panic wherever it appeared. The issues the disease posed for cities and societies during its seven waves of global expansion encapsulate certain primary features and contradictions of the nineteenth century, such as the ambivalence between liberalism and the will of empires for control and regulation.

Cholera arrived for the first time in Western Europe at the beginning of the 1830s and caused a series of dramatic crises in several prominent European cities. Paris was hit hard by the disease in 1832. The epidemic not only jeopardised the sense of confidence of the powerful urban bourgeoisie, but also spurred a series of uprisings that pitted the popular classes against the increasingly influential Parisian elites. When urban space reforms, led by Baron Haussmann, began almost twenty years after the first outbreak of cholera, their main goals were to control precisely the elements that had so shocked Parisian bourgeois elites in the 1830s – cholera and the violent revolt of the poorer classes. Approximately three decades after cholera's first appearance in Paris, Buenos Aires was struck by the disease. The cholera epidemics of 1867–8, which were almost directly followed by a dramatic yellow fever epidemic in

1871, triggered a discussion on the presence of the city's meat-salting factories. These factories polluted a tributary of the River Plate and were deemed responsible by many for the spread of the miasmas at the root of the cholera outbreak. In discussions on the issue, the elites of Buenos Aires also considered options for the future of their city, looking to the model of Paris and other European and North American cities in order to do so, most notably their responses to pollution and epidemic diseases. The urban models the elites of Buenos Aires had in mind were not necessarily realistic; more so than the actual cities themselves, fantasies of European cities such as Paris were the models, the basis of which came to form the bedrock of various projects for Buenos Aires during the discussions held by the city's elites. This does not mean, as is commonly said, that Buenos Aires became the Paris of South America. On the contrary, locally constructed and imagined versions of Paris and other European and North American cities, instead of the 'real Paris', guided the imaginaries of local elites in imagining their city.

If in the section on cholera I reconstructed the influence of Paris on Buenos Aires and characterised it as indirect and sui generis, in the section on the plague, I compared the two cities. The dramatic early modern experience of the plague, which has partly become the quintessential epidemic disease, elicited the establishment of measures and narratives that applied to all epidemics that followed. Whereas the second pandemic is perhaps the most studied series of plague epidemics, the two specific epidemics analysed in the section on the plague pertain to the third plague pandemic. In the last years of the nineteenth century, the plague broke out in Hong Kong, one of the key colonial commercial entrepôts of the British empire at that time. The extreme measures the colonial government enforced as a result of the outbreak primarily targeted the city's Chinese population, who organised protests and resistance en masse. Facing the rebellion of the overwhelming majority of the city's inhabitants, the government was forced to back down from its original course of action. Its attempt to create a distinction between what it deemed the necessary free circulation of ships and goods and the dangerous movements of the Chinese population failed dramatically.

From Hong Kong, the plague arrived in Bombay in 1896, just two years after its first appearance in the Pearl River Delta. By the end of the nineteenth century, Bombay had become one of the most important showcase sites and economic centres of British India. The outbreak of the plague in a city intended to symbolise the modernity of the British civilising mission in the colonies proved to be a blow for the colonial government, which reacted to the epidemic with a series of drastic measures that mainly targeted the workers. These measures drove a great part of the population to flee from Bombay, leaving the city's mills with substantially diminished human resources. The convergence between the resulting enhanced bargaining power of the workers and the protests against the anti-plague measures, which united different ethnic groups for the first time, forced the colonial government and the mill owners to make important concessions to the city's working population. Notwithstanding the different positions occupied by Hong Kong and Bombay in the British empire, in both cases, the plague demonstrated that the colonial administration could not withstand the opposition of the local population without running the risk of losing control and without jeopardising the profitable economic functioning of the two cities.

The section on tuberculosis highlights how the transformation of a widely spread disease into an epidemic, a process that inspires a sense of crisis and the corresponding societal need to intervene, very much depends on the social and cultural comprehension of the disease. Originally considered as pertaining to the fate of the single individual, tuberculosis gradually transformed into a feared epidemic disease at the end of the nineteenth century. The analyses of Baltimore and Buenos Aires provide a comparison of the impact of tuberculosis on the issue of racial, ethnical, and class-based segregation. In Baltimore, tuberculosis, which was closely associated with the African American population in the eyes of a great number of physicians, reinforced the patterns of racial segregation that were already present. Overcrowding and poor living conditions caused by segregation were probably two of the main reasons for the prevalence of the disease among the black population in the city. In a vicious circle, public authorities used tuberculosis to legitimise segregation as a way of protecting other population groups from the infection. If tuberculosis reinforced already existing segregation patterns in Baltimore, it failed to provoke the emergence of ethnical or racial segregation in Buenos Aires. The Argentine capital was not an ethnically segregated city and did not become one in the wake of the rise of fear that accompanied the spread of tuberculosis at the end of the nineteenth century. However, tuberculosis contributed to reinforcing the pre-existing stigmatisation of specific groups of migrants.

Drawing from the single cases presented, this Element has underlined that global processes and events such as pandemics acted in contrasting but nonetheless intersecting ways in distinct urban settings across the globe. The global history of epidemics in cities enables the reconstruction of the history of a variety of wide-reaching entanglements on one hand, which constituted the basic conditions for disease to spread globally. On the other hand, by concentrating on specific urban settings, the global history of epidemics facilitates a greater focus on conflicts, differences, and the unevenness engendered by global entanglements. Diseases that become epidemic – or even pandemic – spread through the lines drawn by human networks across different regions of the world. Epidemics have often been able to challenge and destabilise these networks by making them visible and questionable to contemporaries and thus to historians in retrospect. In other words, for historians interested in the history of connections and disconnections across different regional and national contexts, epidemics can be used as a promising research tool. In fact, like a sort of staining test – to use a biomedical laboratory metaphor – epidemics, which are always also crises of human connections, destabilise networks making them contested and therefore 'stained' and visible. Heuristically, this capacity of epidemics of making human connections visible, along with the specific vantage point cities offer as critical junctures of globalisation that emerge at the conflictual intersection of different scales, promises interesting results for global history.

These results may be of special interest to global historians who intend to engage with the legitimate criticisms recently raised within the field of global history (Adelman 2017; Drayton and Motadel 2018). If global history has been accused of conveying an image of the world as a smooth sphere characterised by converging stories, a focus on epidemics and cities enables showing instead divergences and unevenness in the context of mutual transnational and transregional influences. This Element has focused on epidemics, mainly seeing them through the eyes of a Western genealogy of biomedicine. Furthermore, in order to highlight the social history of epidemics in cities, this Element has dealt only partially with the environmental and inter-species dimension of epidemics, something essential for any global account on the history of health. Future studies might want to take their starting point from different epistemological genealogies of medicine and to explore in greater depth the multifaceted nature of epidemics, not only as social, but also as environmental events.

References

Adelman, Jeremy. 2017. 'What is global history now?' *Aeon*. Accessed 20 October 2021. https://aeon.co/essays/is-global-history-still-possible-or-has-it-had-its-moment.

Ágoston, Gábor. 1998. 'Habsburgs and Ottomans: Defense, military change and shifts in power'. *The Turkish Studies Association Bulletin* 22 (1): 126–41.

Alchon, Suzanne Austin. 2003. *A Pest in the Land: New World Epidemics in a Global Perspective*. Albuquerque: University of New Mexico Press.

Anderson, Warwick. 2006. *Colonial Pathologies: American Tropical Medicine, Race, and Hygiene in the Philippines*. Durham, NC: Duke University Press.

Anderson, Warwick. 1996. 'Immunities of empire: Race, disease, and the new tropical medicine, 1900–1920'. *Bulletin of the History of Medicine* 70 (1): 94–118.

Armus, Diego. 2011. *The Ailing City: Health, Tuberculosis, and Culture in Buenos Aires, 1870–1950*. Durham, NC: Duke University Press.

Armus, Diego, and Adrián López Denis. 2011. 'Disease, medicine, and health'. In *The Oxford Handbook of Latin American History*, edited by Jose C. Moya, 424–53. Oxford: Oxford University Press.

Arnold, David. 1993. *Colonizing the Body: State Medicine and Epidemic Disease in Nineteenth-Century India*. Berkeley: University of California Press.

Arnold, David. 1996. 'Introduction: Tropical medicine before Manson'. In *Warm Climates and Western Medicine: The Emergence of Tropical Medicine*, edited by David Arnold, 1–19. Amsterdam: Rodopi.

Baily, Samuel L. 2000. 'La cadena migratoria de los italianos en la Argentina: Los casos de los agnoneses y siroleses'. In *La inmigración italiana en la Argentina*, edited by Fernando J. Devoto and Diego Armus, 45–62. Buenos Aires: Editorial Biblos.

Baily, Samuel L. 1999. *Immigrants in the Land of Promise: Italians in Buenos Aires and New York City, 1870–1914*. Ithaca, NY: Cornell University Press.

Baldwin, Peter. 1999. *Contagion and the State in Europe, 1830–1930*. Cambridge: Cambridge University Press.

Barnes, David S. 2006. *The Great Stink of Paris and the Nineteenth-Century Struggle against Filth and Germs*. Baltimore, MD: Johns Hopkins University Press.

Barnes, David S. 1995. *The Making of a Social Disease: Tuberculosis in Nineteenth-Century France*. Berkeley: University of California Press.

Bazin, Hervé. 2000. *The Eradication of Smallpox: Edward Jenner and the First and Only Eradication of a Human Infectious Disease*. San Diego, CA: Academic Press.

Benedict, Carol. 1996. *Bubonic Plague in Nineteenth-Century China*. Stanford, CA: Stanford University Press.

Biraben, Jean-Noël. 1975. *Les hommes et la peste en France et dans les pays européens et méditerranéens*. Paris: Mouton.

Birn, Anne-Emmanuelle. 2020. 'Perspectivizing pandemics: (How) do epidemic histories criss-cross contexts?' *Journal of Global History* 15 (3): 336–49.

Birn, Anne-Emmanuelle. 2018. 'Public health and medicine in Latin America'. In *A Global History of Medicine*, edited by Mark Jackson, 118–48. Oxford: Oxford University Press.

Bourdelais, Patrice, and Jean-Yves Raulot. 1987. *Une peure bleue: Histoire du choléra en France, 1832–1854*. Paris: Payot.

Briggs, Asa. 1961. 'Cholera and society in the nineteenth century'. *Past & Present* 19 (1): 76–96.

Brock, Thomas D. 1999. *Robert Koch: A Life in Medicine and Bacteriology*. Washington, DC: ASM Press.

Brook, Timothy. 2020. 'Comparative pandemics: The Tudor–Stuart and Wanli–Chongzhen years of pestilence, 1567–1666'. *Journal of Global History* 15 (3): 363–79.

Cagle, Hugh. 2018. *Assembling the Tropics: Science and Medicine in Portugal's Empire, 1450–1700*. Cambridge: Cambridge University Press.

Calvi, Giulia. 1989. *Histories of a Plague Year: The Social and the Imaginary in Baroque Florence*. Berkeley: University of California Press.

Campbell, Margaret. 2005. 'What tuberculosis did for modernism: The influence of a curative environment on modernist design and architecture'. *Medical History* 49 (4): 463–88.

Cantor, Norman F. 2001. *In the Wake of the Plague: The Black Death and the World It Made*. New York: Free Press.

Carbone, Antonio. 2022a. *Park, Tenement, Slaughterhouse: Elite Imaginaries of Buenos Aires, 1852–1880*. Frankfurt: Campus.

Carbone, Antonio. 2022b. 'Provincializing industry: Hyperreal urban modernity in nineteenth-century Buenos Aires'. In *European Cities: Modernity, Race and Colonialism*, edited by Noa K. Ha and Giovanni Picker, 77–96. Manchester: Manchester University Press.

Carlino, Andrea. 1999. *Books of the Body: Anatomical Ritual and Renaissance Learning*. Chicago: University of Chicago Press.

Carmichael, Ann G. 1986. *Plague and the Poor in Renaissance Florence*. Cambridge: Cambridge University Press.

Chakrabarti, Pratik. 2014. *Medicine and Empire: 1600–1960*. Basingstoke: Palgrave Macmillan.

Chalhoub, Sidney. 1993. 'The politics of disease control: Yellow fever and race in nineteenth-century Rio De Janeiro, Brazil'. *Journal of Latin American Studies* 25 (3): 441–63.

Chevalier, Louis. 1973. *Labouring Classes and Dangerous Classes: In Paris during the First Half of the Nineteenth Century*. London: Routledge.

Chu, Cecilia. 2013. 'Combating nuisance: Sanitation, regulation, and the politics of property in colonial Hong Kong'. In *Imperial Contagions: Medicine, Hygiene, and Cultures of Planning in Asia*, edited by Robert S. Peckham and David M. Pomfret, 17–36. Hong Kong: Hong Kong University Press.

Cipolla, Carlo. 1981. *Fighting the Plague in Seventeenth-Century Italy*. Madison: University of Wisconsin Press.

Cleere, Eileen. 2016. *Sanitary Arts: Aesthetic Culture and the Victorian Cleanliness Campaigns*. Columbus: Ohio State University Press.

Cohn, Samuel. 2018. *Epidemics: Hate and Compassion from the Plague of Athens to AIDS*. Oxford: Oxford University Press.

Cook, Harold J. 2018. 'Medicine in Western Europe'. In *A Global History of Medicine*, edited by Mark Jackson, 44–68. Oxford: Oxford University Press.

Cooper, Frederick. 2001. 'What is the concept of globalization good for? An African historian's perspective'. *African Affairs* 100 (399): 189–213.

Corbin, Alain. 1986. *The Foul and the Fragrant: Odor and the French Social Imagination*. Cambridge, MA: Harvard University Press.

Crawshaw, Jane L. Stevens. 2012. *Plague Hospitals: Public Health for the City in Early Modern Venice*. Aldershot: Ashgate.

Curtin, Philip D. 1989. *Death by Migration: Europe's Encounter with the Tropical World in the Nineteenth Century*. Cambridge: Cambridge University Press.

Curtin, Philip D. 1990. 'The end of the "White Man's Grave"? Nineteenth-century mortality in West Africa'. *Journal of Interdisciplinary History* 21 (1): 63–88.

Curtin, Philip D. 1985. 'Medical knowledge and urban planning in tropical Africa'. *The American Historical Review* 90 (3): 594–613.

Daston, Lorraine, and Peter Galison. 2007. *Objectivity*. New York: Zone.

Day, Carolyn A. 2017. *Consumptive Chic: A History of Beauty, Fashion, and Disease*. London: Bloomsbury Academic.

Delaporte, François. 1986. *Disease and Civilization: The Cholera in Paris, 1832*. Cambridge, MA: MIT Press.

Drayton, Richard, and David Motadel. 2018. 'Discussion: The futures of global history'. *Journal of Global History* 13 (1): 1–21.

Durey, Michael. 1979. *The Return of the Plague: British Society and the Cholera 1831–2*. Dublin: Gill and Macmillan.

Ebrahimnejad, Hormoz. 2018. 'Medicine in Islam and Islamic medicine'. In *A Global History of Medicine*, edited by Mark Jackson, 69–95. Oxford: Oxford University Press.

Echenberg, Myron J. 2007. *Plague Ports: The Global Urban Impact of Bubonic Plague, 1894–1901*. New York: New York University Press.

Eisenberg, Merle, and Lee Mordechai. 2020. 'The Justinianic Plague and global pandemics: The making of the plague concept'. *The American Historical Review* 125 (5): 1632–67.

Evans, Richard. 1987. *Death in Hamburg: Society and Politics in the Cholera Years 1830–1910*. Oxford: Clarendon.

Evans, Richard. 1988. 'Epidemic and revolutions: Cholera in nineteenth-century Europe'. *Past & Present* 120: 123–46.

Fiquepron, Maximiliano. 2020. *Morir en las grandes pestes: Las epidemias de cólera y fiebre amarilla en la Buenos Aires del siglo XIX*. Buenos Aires: Siglo XXI Editores.

Foucault, Michel. 2007. *Security, Territory, Population: Lectures at the Collège De France, 1977–78*. Basingstoke: Palgrave Macmillan.

Fuchs, Thomas. 2001. *The Mechanization of the Heart: Harvey and Descartes*. Rochester, NY: University of Rochester Press.

Gandy, Matthew. 2014. *The Fabric of Space: Water, Modernity, and the Urban Imagination*. Cambridge, MA: MIT Press.

Gaynes, Robert P. 2011. *Germ Theory: Medical Pioneers in Infectious Diseases*. Washington, DC: ASM Press.

Goebel, Michael. 2016. 'All things transregional? In conversation with . . . Michael Goebel'. Accessed 18 October 2021. https://trafo.hypotheses.org/4455.

Goebel, Michael. 2018. 'A metropolitan world'. *Aeon*: Accessed 18 October 2021. https://aeon.co/essays/intellectual-life-is-still-catching-up-to-urbanisation.

Green, Monica H. 2020a. 'Emerging diseases, re-emerging histories'. *Centaurus* 62: 234–47.

Green, Monica H. 2020b. 'The four Black Deaths'. *The American Historical Review* 125 (5): 1601–31.

Gutiérrez, Ramón. 2013. 'Buenos Aires: A great European city'. In *Planning Latin America's Capital Cities 1850–1950*, edited by Arturo Almandoz, 45–74. Abingdon: Routledge.

Halliday, Stephen. 2001. *The Great Stink of London: Sir Joseph Bazalgette and the Cleansing of the Victorian Capital*. Stroud: Sutton.

Hamlin, Christopher. 2009. *Cholera: The Biography*. Oxford: Oxford University Press.

Hamlin, Christopher. 1998. *Public Health and Social Justice in the Age of Chadwick*. Cambridge: Cambridge University Press.

Hannaway, Caroline, and Ann La Berg, eds. 1998. *Constructing Paris Medicine*. Amsterdam: Rodopi.

Harrison, Mark. 1999. *Climates and Constitutions: Health, Race, Environment and British Imperialism in India 1600–1850*. Oxford: Oxford University Press.

Harrison, Mark. 2012. *Contagion: How Commerce Has Spread Disease*. New Haven, CT: Yale University Press.

Harrison, Mark. 2018. 'The great shift: Cholera theory and sanitary policy in British India, 1867–1879'. In *Society, Medicine and Politics in Colonial India*, edited by Biswamoy Pati and Mark Harrison, 37–60. London: Routledge.

Harrison, Mark. 2010. *Medicine in an Age of Commerce and Empire: Britain and Its Tropical Colonies*. Oxford: Oxford University Press.

Hayden, Dolores. 2003. *Building Suburbia: Green Fields and Urban Growth, 1820–2000*. New York: Pantheon.

Hays, Jo N. 2007. 'Historians and epidemics: Simple questions, complex answers'. In *Plague and the End of Antiquity: The Pandemic of 541–750*, edited by Lester K. Little, 35–56. Cambridge: Cambridge University Press.

Herlihy, David. 1997. *The Black Death and the Transformation of the West*. Cambridge, MA: Harvard University Press.

Hernández Sáenz, Luz María. 1997. *Learning to Heal: The Medical Profession in Colonial Mexico 1767–1831*. New York: Lang.

Huber, Valeska. 2013. *Channelling Mobilities: Migration and Globalisation in the Suez Canal Region and Beyond, 1869–1914*. Cambridge: Cambridge University Press.

Huber, Valeska. 2020. 'Pandemics and the politics of difference: Rewriting the history of internationalism through nineteenth-century cholera'. *Journal of Global History* 15 (3): 394–407.

Humphreys, Peter. 1989. 'The Magic Mountain: A time capsule of tuberculosis treatment in the early twentieth century'. *Canadian Bulletin of Medical History – Bulletin Canadien d'Histoire de la Médecine* 6 (2): 147–63.

Jackson, Mark, ed. 2018. *A Global History of Medicine*. Oxford: Oxford University Press.

Jackson, Mark. 2018. 'One world, one health? Towards a global history of medicine'. In *A Global History of Medicine*, edited by Mark Jackson, 1–18. Oxford: Oxford University Press.

Jordan, David P. 1995. *Transforming Paris: The Life and Labors of Baron Haussmann*. New York: Free Press.

Jouanna, Jacques. 2012. 'Air, miasma and contagion in the time of Hippocrates and the survival of miasmas in post-Hippocratic medicine (Rufus of Ephesus, Galen and Palladius)'. In *Greek Medicine from Hippocrates to Galen: Selected Papers*, edited by Jacques Jouanna, Philip van der Eijk, and Neil Allies, 119–36. Leiden: Brill.

Joyce, Patrick. 2003. *The Rule of Freedom: Liberalism and the Modern City*. London: Verso.

Kirkland, Stephane. 2013. *Paris Reborn: Napoléon III, Baron Haussmann, and the Quest to Build a Modern City*. New York: Picador.

Kudlick, Catherine Jean. 1996. *Cholera in Post-Revolutionary Paris: A Cultural History*. Berkeley: University of California Press.

Landwehr, Achim. 2012. 'Die Kunst, sich nicht allzu sicher zu sein: Möglichkeiten kritischer Geschichtsschreibung'. Accessed 20 October 2021. https://werkstattgeschichte.de/wp-content/uploads/2016/08/WG61_007-014_LANDWEHR_KUNST.pdf.

Latour, Bruno. 1988. *The Pasteurization of France*. Cambridge, MA: Harvard University Press.

Little, Lester K. 2007. 'Life and afterlife of the first plague pandemic'. In *Plague and the End of Antiquity: The Pandemic of 541–750*, edited by Lester K. Little, 3–32. Cambridge: Cambridge University Press.

Little, Lester K., ed. 2007. *Plague and the End of Antiquity: The Pandemic of 541–750*. Cambridge: Cambridge University Press.

Lo, Vivienne, and Michael Stanley-Baker. 2018. 'Chinese medicine'. In *A Global History of Medicine*, edited by Mark Jackson, 19–43. Oxford: Oxford University Press.

McGrew, Roderick E. 1965. *Russia and the Cholera: 1823–1832*. Madison: University of Wisconsin Press.

McMillen, Christian W. 2015. *Discovering Tuberculosis: A Global History, 1900 to the Present*. New Haven, CT: Yale University Press.

McNeill, John Robert. 2010. *Mosquito Empires: Ecology and War in the Greater Caribbean, 1620–1914*. Cambridge: Cambridge University Press.

McNeill, William. 1998. *Plagues and Peoples*. New York: Anchor Books.

Melosi, Martin V. 2000. *The Sanitary City: Urban Infrastructure in America from Colonial Times to the Present*. Baltimore, MD: Johns Hopkins University Press.

Middell, Matthias, and Katja Naumann. 2010. 'Global history and the spatial turn: From the impact of area studies to the study of critical junctures of globalization'. *Journal of Global History* 5 (1): 149–70.

Moote, Alanson Lloyd, and Dorothy C. Moote. 2004. *The Great Plague: The Story of London's Most Deadly Year*. Baltimore, MD: Johns Hopkins University Press.

Moya, José C. 1998. *Cousins and Strangers: Spanish Immigrants in Buenos Aires, 1850–1930*. Berkeley: University of California Press.

Nightingale, Carl H. 2012. *Segregation: A Global History of Divided Cities*. Chicago: University of Chicago Press.

Nutton, Vivian. 2013. *Ancient Medicine*. Abingdon: Routledge.

Osborne, Michael A. 1996. 'Resurrecting Hippocrates: Hygienic sciences and the French scientific expeditions to Egypt, Morea and Algeria'. In *Warm Climates and Western Medicine: The Emergence of Tropical Medicine*, edited by David Arnold, 80–98. Amsterdam: Rodopi.

Packard, Randall M. 2007. *Making of a Tropical Disease*. Baltimore, MD: Johns Hopkins University Press.

Papagrigorakis, Manolis J., Christos Yapijakis, Philippos N. Synodinos, and Effie Baziotopoulou-Valavani. 2006. 'DNA examination of ancient dental pulp incriminates typhoid fever as a probable cause of the Plague of Athens'. *International Journal of Infectious Diseases* 10 (3): 206–14.

Park, Sun-Young. 2018. *Ideals of the Body: Architecture, Urbanism, and Hygiene in Postrevolutionary Paris*. Pittsburgh, PA: University of Pittsburgh Press.

Peckham, Robert. 2016. *Epidemics in Modern Asia*. Cambridge: Cambridge University Press.

Puiggari, Miguel. 1871. *Sobre la inocuidad de los saladeros*. Buenos Aires: Imprenta de La Tribuna.

Ramsden, Edmud. 2018. 'Science and medicine in the United States of America'. In *A Global History of Medicine*, edited by Mark Jackson, 149–72. Oxford: Oxford University Press.

Roberts, Samuel. 2009. *Infectious Fear: Politics, Disease, and the Health Effects of Segregation*. Chapel Hill: University of North Carolina Press.

Rosenberg, Charles E. 1989. 'What is an epidemic? AIDS in historical perspective'. *Dedalus* 118 (2): 1–17.

Ruestow, Edward G. 1996. *The Microscope in the Dutch Republic: The Shaping of Discovery*. Cambridge: Cambridge University Press.

Sarasin, Philipp. 2001. *Reizbare Maschinen: Eine Geschichte des Körpers 1765–1914*. Frankfurt: Suhrkamp.

Sarkar, Aditya. 2014. 'The tie that snapped: Bubonic plague and mill labour in Bombay, 1896–1898'. *International Review of Social History* 59 (2): 181–214.

Scheidel, Walter. 2018. *The Great Leveler: Violence and the History of Inequality from the Stone Age to the Twenty-First Century*. Princeton, NJ: Princeton University Press.

Scobie, James R. 1992. *Buenos Aires: Plaza to Suburbs, 1870–1910*. Oxford: Oxford University Press.

Sluyter, Andrew. 2010. 'The Hispanic Atlantic's tasajo trail'. *Latin American Research Review* 45 (1): 98–120.

Snowden, Frank M. 2006. *The Conquest of Malaria: Italy, 1900–1962*. New Haven, CT: Yale University Press.

Snowden, Frank M. 2019. *Epidemics and Society: From the Black Death to the Present*. New Haven, CT: Yale University Press.

Sontag, Susan. 1978. *Illness As Metaphor*. New York: Farrar, Straus and Giroux.

Tagliacozzo, Eric. 2013. *The Longest Journey: Southeast Asians and the Pilgrimage to Mecca*. Oxford: Oxford University Press.

Talty, Stephan. 2009. *The Illustrious Dead: The Terrifying Story of How Typhus Killed Napoleon's Greatest Army*. New York: Crown.

Taunton, Matthew. 2009. *Fictions of the City: Class, Culture and Mass Housing in London and Paris*. Basingstoke: Palgrave Macmillan.

Tomes, Nancy. 1999. *The Gospel of Germs: Men, Women, and the Microbe in American Life*. Cambridge, MA: Harvard University Press.

Volf, Élie, and Jean-Jacques Aulas. 2019. *L'homéopathie de Samuel Hahnemann à Luc Montagnier: Mémoire de l'eau, placebo et molécules virtuelles*. Paris: L'Harmattan.

Warner, John H. 2003. *Against the Spirit of System: The French Impulse in Nineteenth-Century American Medicine*. Baltimore, MD: Johns Hopkins University Press.

Watts, Sheldon J. 1999. *Epidemics and History: Disease, Power and Imperialism*. New Haven, CT: Yale University Press.

Weisz, George. 2001. 'Reconstructing Paris medicine: Essay review'. *Bulletin of the History of Medicine* 75 (1): 105–20.

Whittles, Lilith K., and Xavier Didelot. 2016. 'Epidemiological analysis of the Eyam plague outbreak of 1665–1666'. *Proceedings. Biological Sciences* 283 (1830): 1–9. http://dx.doi.org/10.1098/rspb.2016.0618.

Williams, Raymond. 1973. *The Country and the City*. London: Chatto & Windus.

Yip, Ka-che, Yuansheng Liang, and Wenjiang Huang. 2016. *Health Policy and Disease in Colonial and Postcolonial Hong Kong, 1841–2003*. London: Routledge.

Zeheter, Michael. 2016. *Epidemics, Empire, and Environments: Cholera in Madras and Quebec City, 1818–1910*. Pittsburgh, PA: University of Pittsburgh Press.

Global Urban History

Michael Goebel

Graduate Institute Geneva

Michael Goebel is the Pierre du Bois Chair Europe and the World and Associate Professor of International History at the Graduate Institute Geneva. His research focuses on the histories of nationalism, of cities, and of migration. He is the author of *Anti-imperial Metropolis: Interwar Paris and the Seeds of Third World Nationalism* (2015).

Tracy Neumann

Wayne State University

Tracy Neumann is an Associate Professor of History at Wayne State University. Her research focuses on global and transnational approaches to cities and the built environment. She is the author of *Remaking the Rust Belt: The Postindustrial Transformation of North America* (2016) and of essays on urban history and public policy.

Joseph Ben Prestel

Freie Universität Berlin

Joseph Ben Prestel is an Assistant Professor (wissenschaftlicher Mitarbeiter) of history at Freie Universität Berlin. His research focuses on the histories of Europe and the Middle East in the nineteenth and twentieth centuries as well as on global and urban history. He is the author of *Emotional Cities: Debates on Urban Change in Berlin and Cairo, 1860–1910* (2017).

About the Series

This series proposes a new understanding of urban history by reinterpreting the history of the world's cities. While urban history has tended to produce single-city case studies, global history has mostly been concerned with the interconnectedness of the world. Combining these two approaches produces a new framework to think about the urban past. The individual titles in the series emphasize global, comparative, and transnational approaches. They deliver empirical research about specific cities, while also exploring questions that expand the narrative outside the immediate locale to give insights into global trends and conceptual debates. Authored by established and emerging scholars whose work represents the most exciting new directions in urban history, this series makes pioneering research accessible to specialists and non-specialists alike.

Cambridge Elements $\equiv$

Global Urban History

Printed in the United States
by Baker & Taylor Publisher Services